ALPHABETIC PHONICS
FAST START FOR EARLY READERS LEVEL 1

Written and illustrated by Paul Mackie.
Cover Picture graphic: - shutterstock

Library and Archives Canada Cataloguing in Publication

Mackie, Paul - Author
ALPHABETIC PHONICS
FAST START FOR EARLY READERS LEVEL 1

ISBN 978-1-988986-12-8

Copyright© 2019 by Paul Mackie

All rights reserved. No part of this book may be reproduced, or utilized in any form, or by any means, electronic, mechanical or photocopying (unless stated in this book), without permission in writing from the Author.
Contact author: **educationalchildsplay@gmail.com**

http://howtoteachchildrentoread.ca

The methods presented in this book are intended to help children learn how to read and are not a guarantee of success that a child will learn how to read or write.

All methods in this book are the ideas of the author and do not represent the views of other books, authors and their methods.

Contents

SHORT SENTENCE READERS	5
LETTER "a"	8
LETTER "b"	10
LETTER "c"	12
LETTER "d"	14
LETTER "e"	16
LETTER "f"	18
LETTER "g"	20
LETTER "h"	22
LETTER "i"	24
LETTER "j"	26
LETTER "k"	28
LETTER "l"	30
LETTER "m"	32
LETTER "n"	34
LETTER "o"	36
LETTER "p"	38
LETTER "q"	40
LETTER "r"	42
LETTER "s"	44
LETTER "t"	46
LETTER "u"	48
LETTER "v"	50
LETTER "w"	52
LETTER "x"	54
LETTER "y"	56
LETTER "z"	58
LETTER SOUNDS – SIGHT WORDS "a"	60
LETTER SOUNDS – SIGHT WORDS "b"	61

LETTER SOUNDS – SIGHT WORDS "c" 62
LETTER SOUNDS – SIGHT WORDS "d" 63
LETTER SOUNDS – SIGHT WORDS "e" 64
LETTER SOUNDS – SIGHT WORDS "f" 65
LETTER SOUNDS – SIGHT WORDS "g" 66
LETTER SOUNDS – SIGHT WORDS "h" 67
LETTER SOUNDS – SIGHT WORDS "i" 68
LETTER SOUNDS – SIGHT WORDS "j" 69
LETTER SOUNDS – SIGHT WORDS "k" 70
LETTER SOUNDS – SIGHT WORDS "l" 71
LETTER SOUNDS – SIGHT WORDS "m" 72
LETTER SOUNDS – SIGHT WORDS "n" 73
LETTER SOUNDS – SIGHT WORDS "o" 74
LETTER SOUNDS – SIGHT WORDS "p" 75
LETTER SOUNDS – SIGHT WORDS "q" 76
LETTER SOUNDS – SIGHT WORDS "r" 77
LETTER SOUNDS – SIGHT WORDS "s" 78
LETTER SOUNDS – SIGHT WORDS "t" 79
LETTER SOUNDS – SIGHT WORDS "u" 80
LETTER SOUNDS – SIGHT WORDS "v" 81
LETTER SOUNDS – SIGHT WORDS "w" 82
LETTER SOUNDS – SIGHT WORDS "x" 83
LETTER SOUNDS – SIGHT WORDS "y" 84
LETTER SOUNDS – SIGHT WORDS "z" 85
OTHER BOOKS BY THE AUTHOR 86
ABOUT THE AUTHOR 91

SHORT SENTENCE READERS

Early Readers: Start with a single word; then two words or more; all words should be lowercase letters and where possible be able to be sounded out phonetically; pictures should be black and white, or a color picture without a background.

Storybooks: are usually in color and should have Sight Words and three or four-letter words that can be sounded out phonetically, where possible.

SHORT SENTENCE READERS

Once a pre-school child has learned the 26-alphabet letter sounds, 60 phonogram blended consonant sounds and the Pre-primer Sight Words, it is time to introduce short sentence readers of two, three, four or more words.

Short sentence readers for beginner readers should be black and white line drawings, so as not to distract the pre-school reader. The words are usually two then three and four-word sentences that can where possible be sounded out phonetically, with a CVC (Consonant – Vowel – Consonant) to make the word; sentences are usually a noun (name of something), a verb (an action), or a sight word.

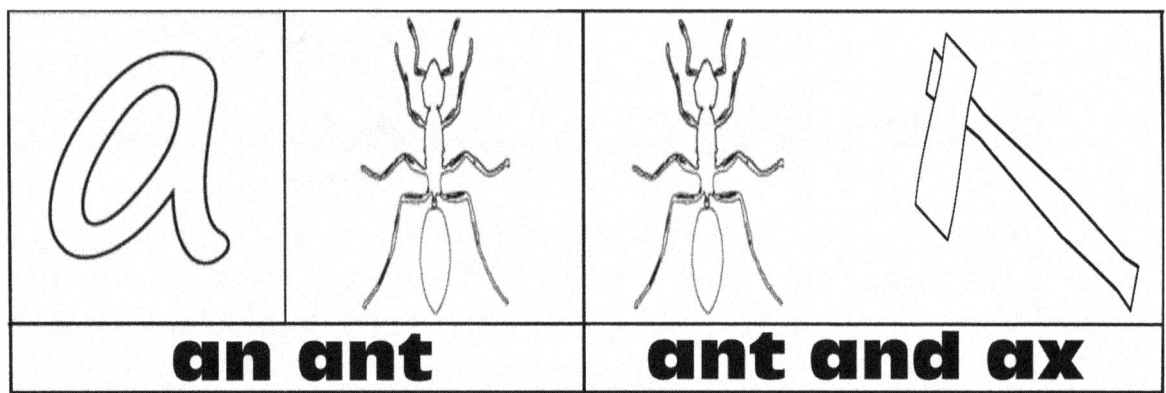

Early reader storybooks can be color with short two, three, or four-letter words using the 26 phonetic alphabet sounds and minimal sight words.

NOTE: It is said that babies see black and white easier; seeing color is said to develop around 6 months of age or older.

The sentences do not necessarily have to make sense; the child should be able to read and pronounce the letter sounds; and recognize the Pre- Primer Sight Words.

Play Based Ways To Teach Your Child To Read
- Have your child point to each letter in the words and sound them out.
- Point to each word and ask your child, "What word is this?"
- Point to each word quickly and ask your child to say the word.

Some letters such as "q" (usually written as "qu") may not be able to be sounded out phonetically with their single lowercase letter sound.

Some words in this book may not be able to be sounded out phonetically because of their spelling and should be taught as sight words.

SHORT SENTENCE READERS

Where possible, this book presents the 26 phonetic letter sounds of the alphabet, and some of the pre-primer Sight Words to make short sentences.

Pre-primer: (40 words) a, and, away, big, blue, can, come, down, find, for, funny, go, help, here, I, in, is, it, jump, little, look, make, me, my, not, one, play, red, run, said, see, the, three, to, two, up, we, where, yellow, you.

Primer: (52 words) all, am, are, at, ate, be, black, brown, but, came, did, do, eat, four, get, good, have, he, into, like, must, new, no, now, on, our, out, please, pretty, ran, ride, saw, say, she, so, soon, that, there, they, this, too, under, want, was, well, went, what, white, who, will, with, yes.

Short sentence readers are best in a step by step progressive order:

- Two words which have three or four letters that can be sounded out phonetically (their lowercase letter sound); no punctuation or capitals.
- Three words which have three or four letters that can be sounded out phonetically: no punctuation or capitals.
- Four words which have three, four or more letters that can be sounded out phonetically with punctuation, capitals and sight words.
- Introduction of pre and primer (up to 5 years) sight words that cannot be sounded out phonetically.
- Complete sentences with sight words, capitals and punctuation.

FAST START FOR EARLY READERS – Level 1, has two and three - word sentences, with no punctuation; and where possible, words that can be sounded out with their lowercase phonetic sound; sight words are only used where necessary to make a sentence, and where no picture is available.

FAST START FOR EARLY READERS – Level 2, has four or more word punctuated and capitalized sentences; words with blended consonant and vowel sounds; words with pre and primer sight words to make short sentences.

Note: Some letters such as "s" can have different phonetic letter sounds, depending where the letter is in a word; words such as "sun", "mess" or "his", while the "s" is the same letter, they have different phonetic sounds.

LETTER "a"

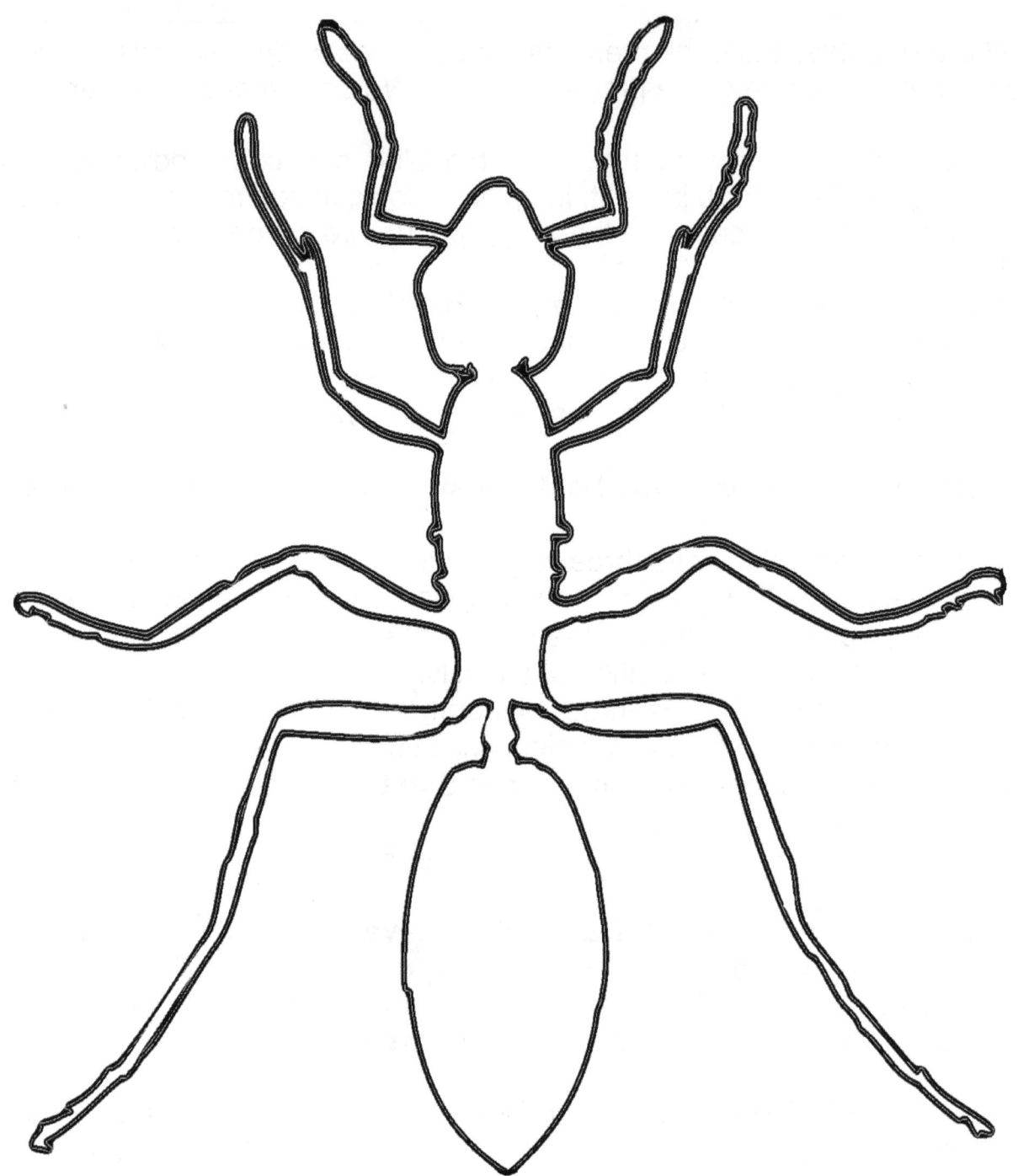

an ant

LETTER "a"

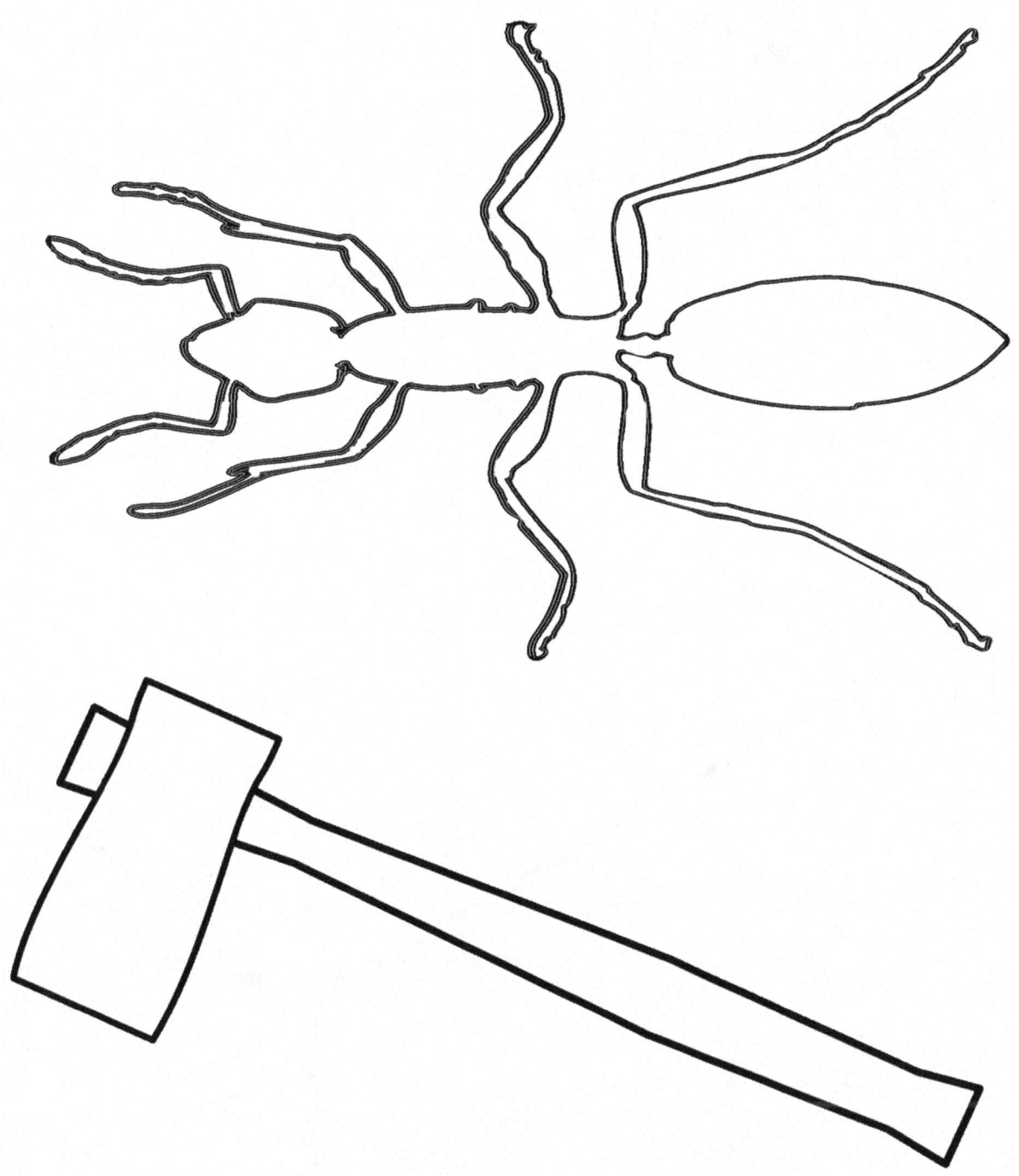

ant and axe

LETTER "b"

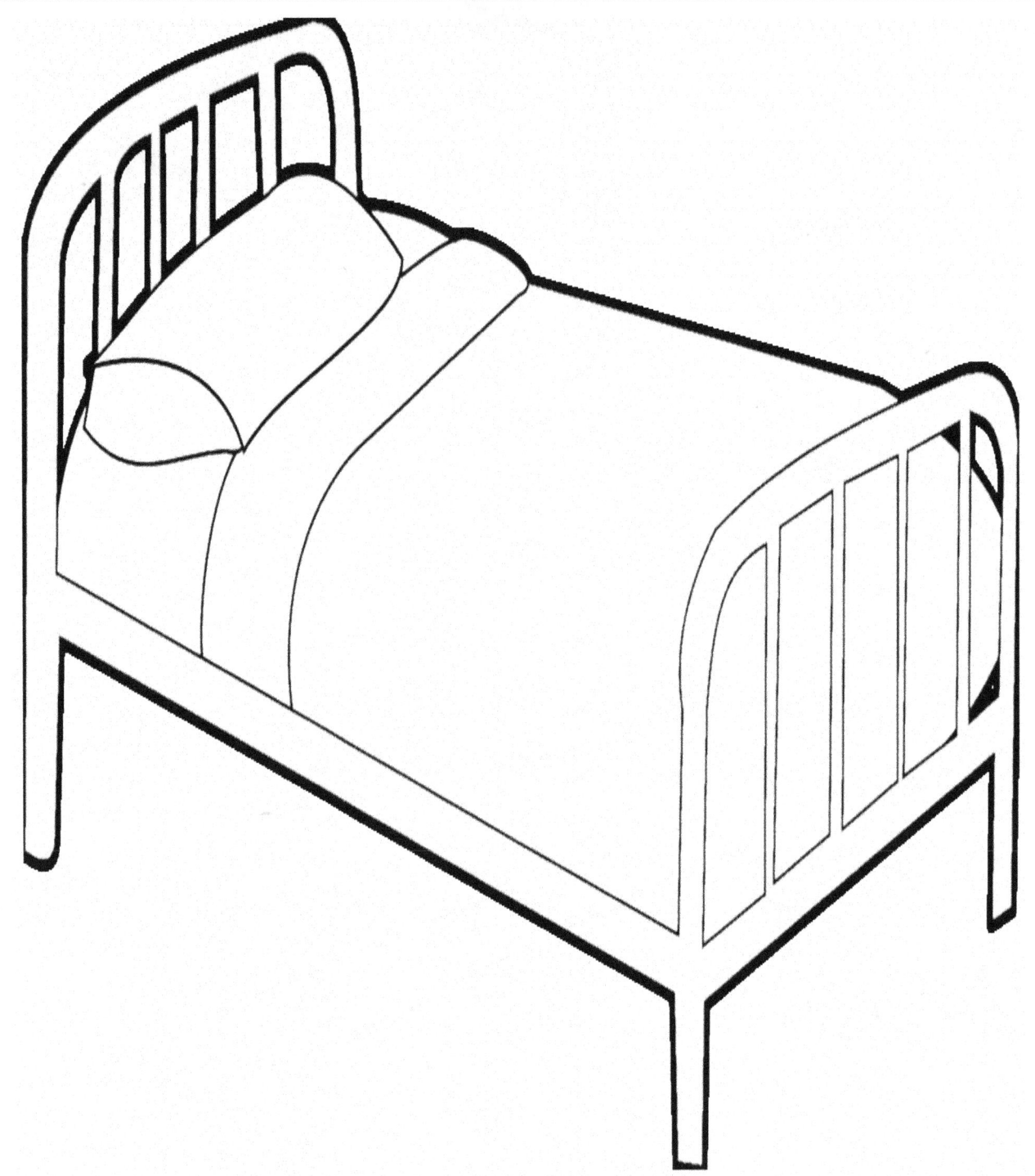

big bed

LETTER "b"

big black bed

LETTER "c"

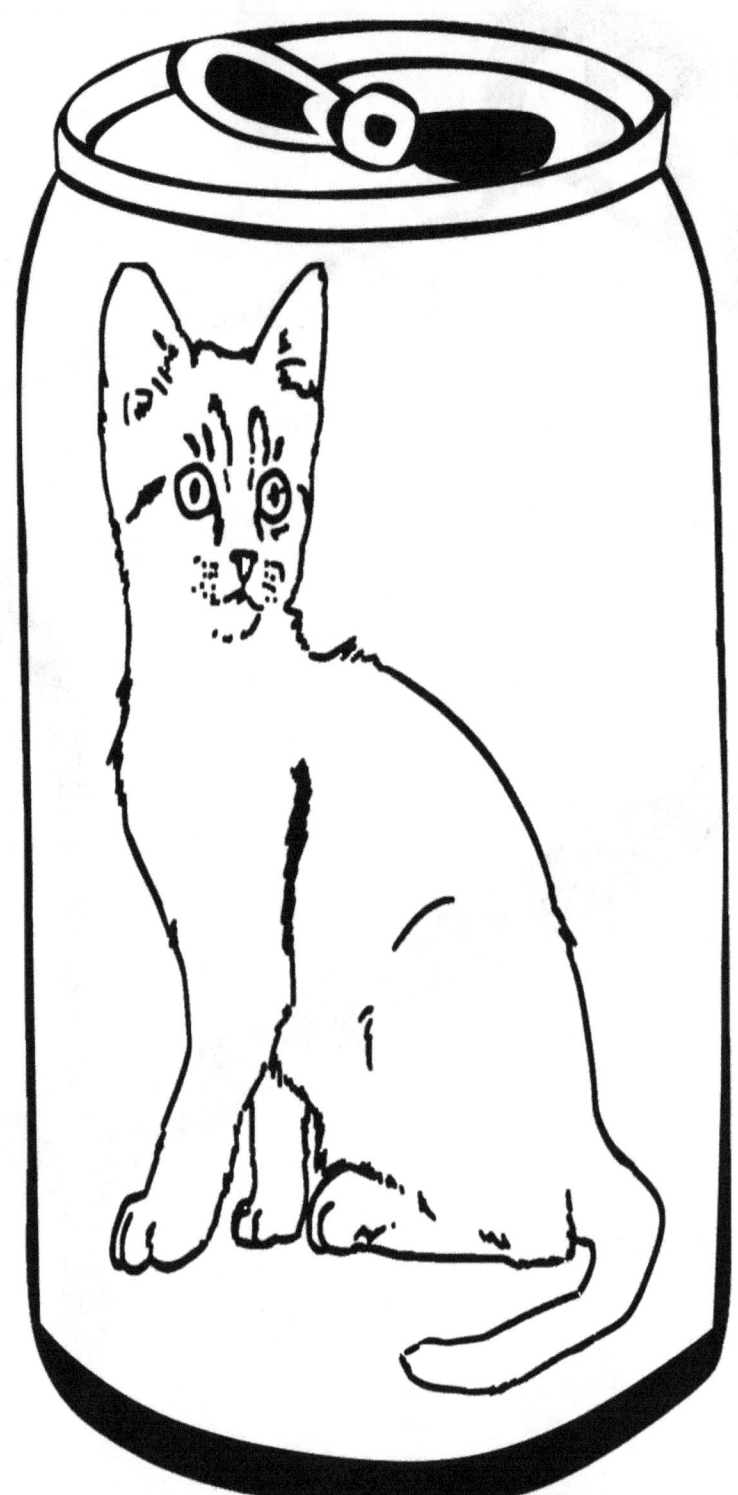

cat can

LETTER "c"

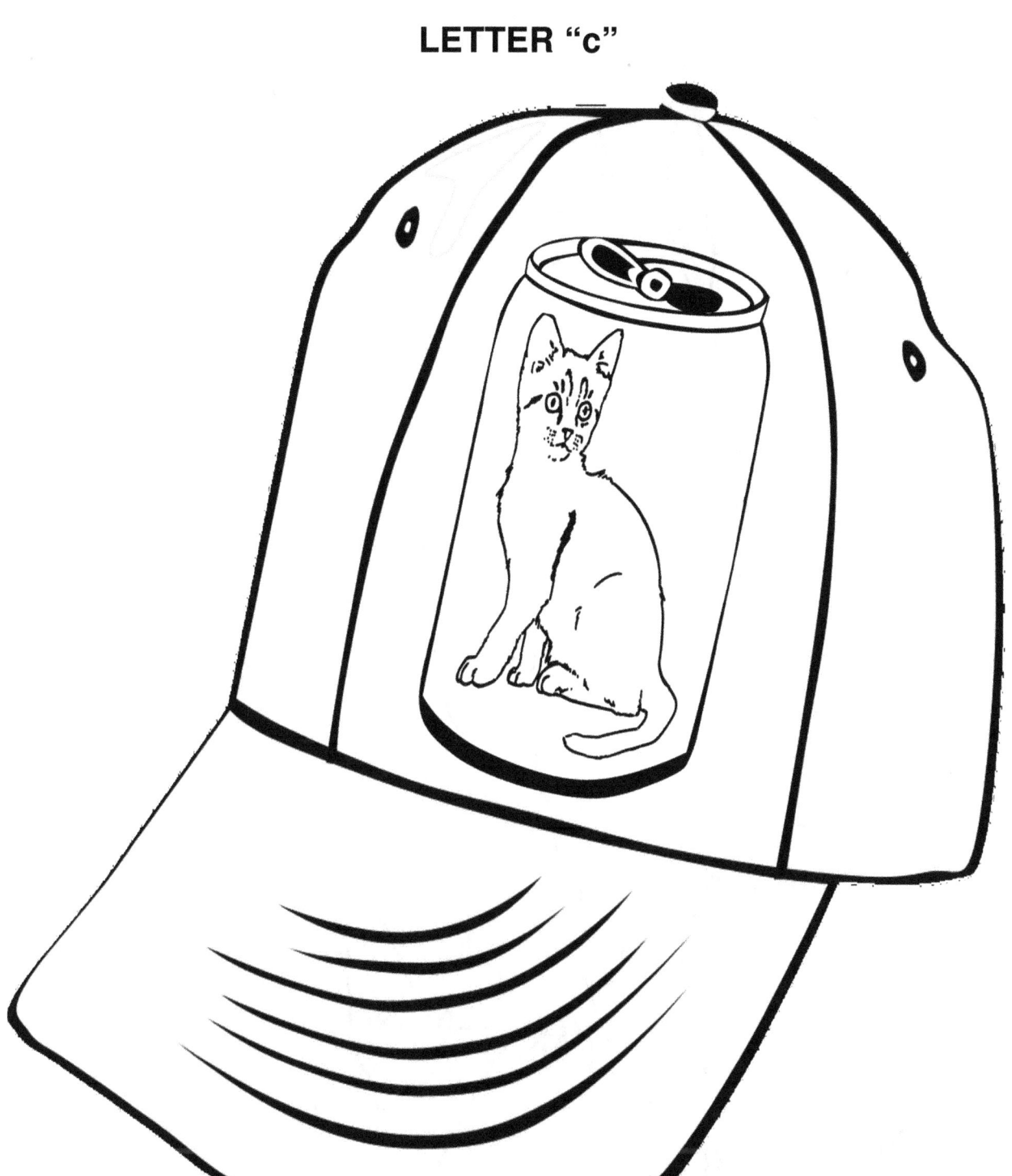

cat can cap

LETTER "d"

dog digs

LETTER "d"

did dad dig

LETTER "e"

extra egg

LETTER "e"

elks egg ends

LETTER "f"

fat frog

LETTER "f"

fit frogs flip

LETTER "g"

get gas

LETTER "g"

gran gets gum

LETTER "h"

hot hat

LETTER "h"

his hot hut

LETTER "i"

in ink

LETTER "i"

is it igloo

LETTER "j"

jug jam

LETTER "j"

jet jabs jello

LETTER "k"

kiss kitten

LETTER "k"

kid kicks keg

LETTER "l"

left log

LETTER "l"

lit lamp low

LETTER "m"

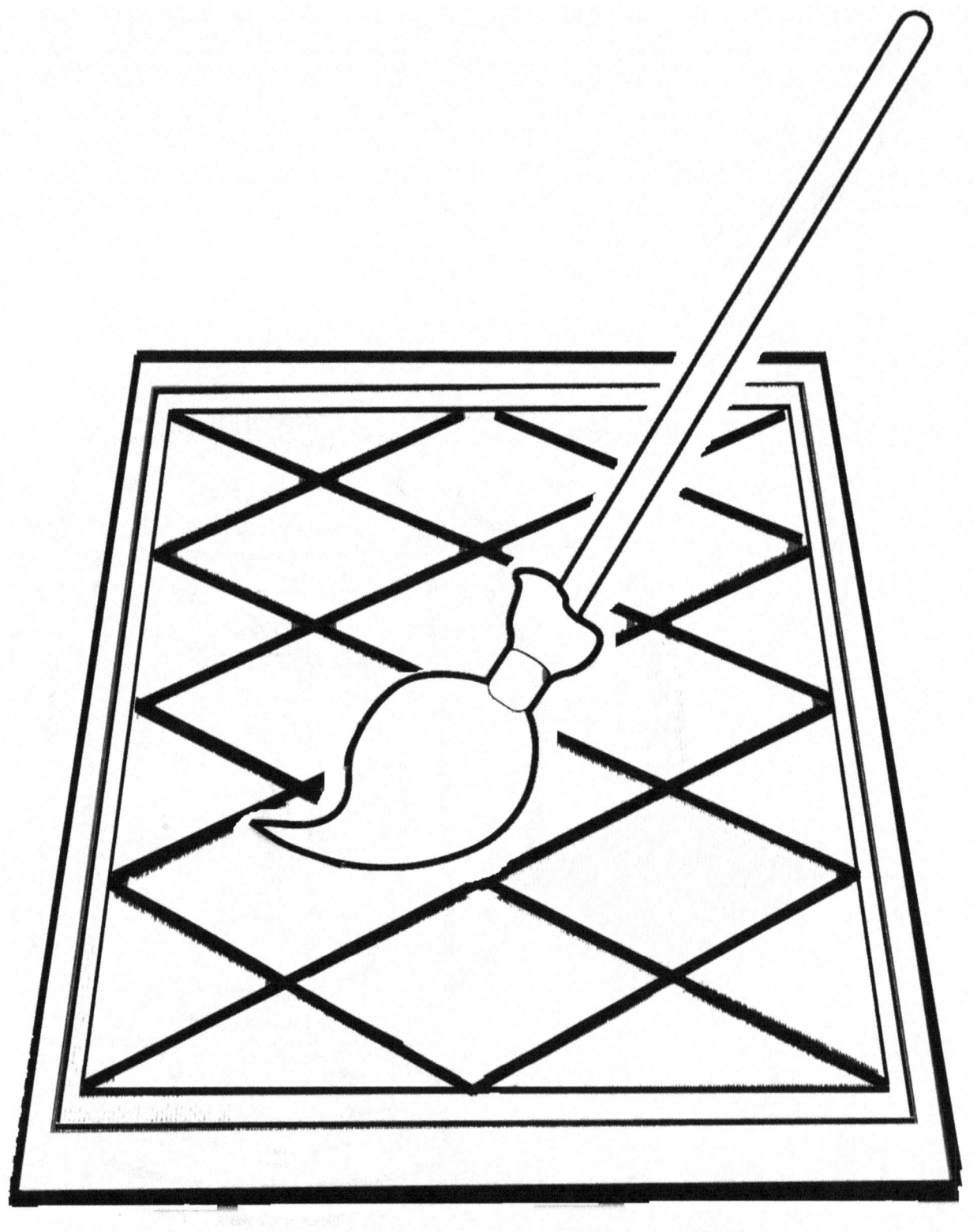

mop mat

LETTER "m"

moms milk mugs

LETTER "n"

next nun

LETTER "n"

nab nut now

LETTER "o"

on otter

LETTER "o"

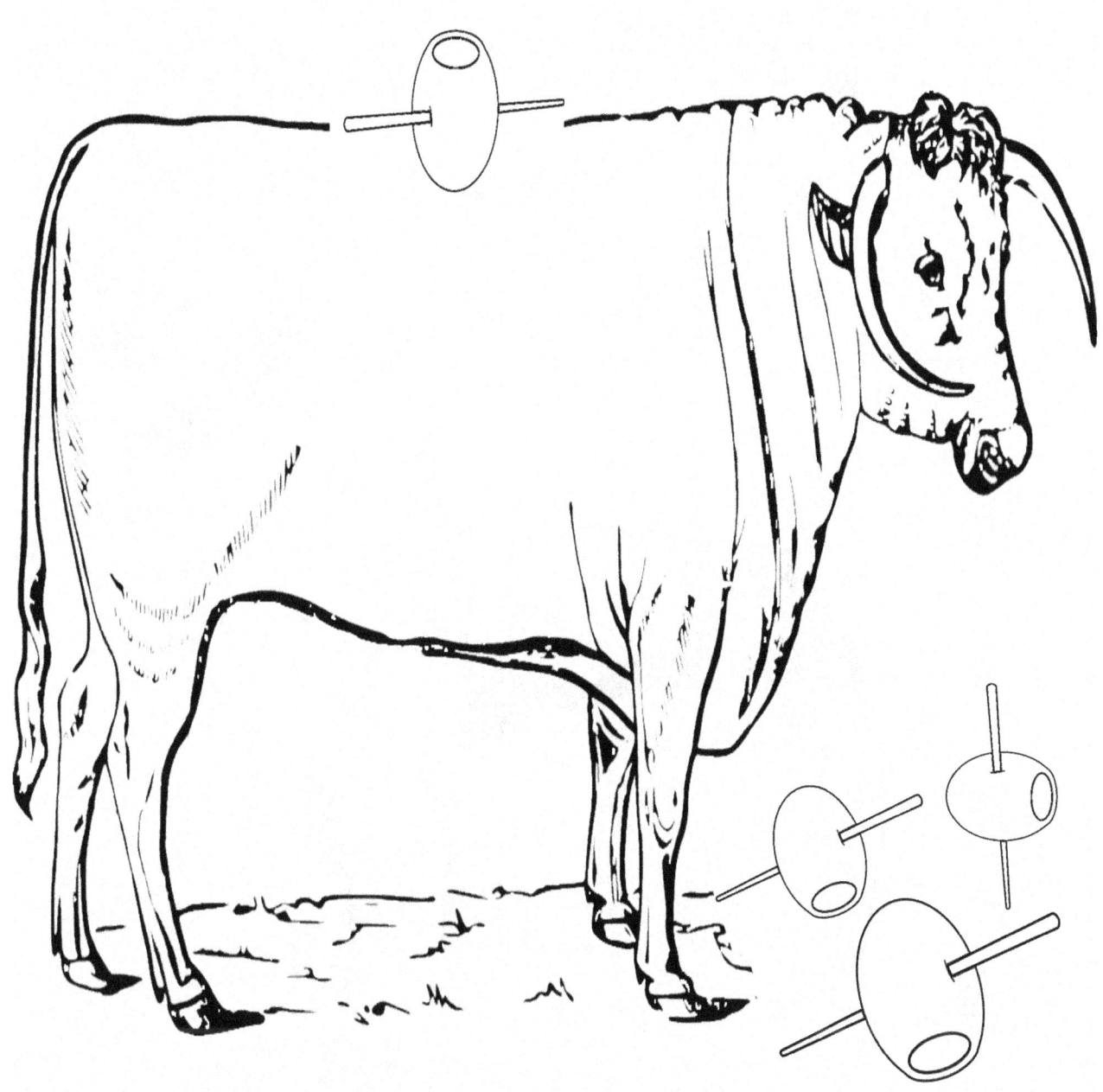

olive on ox

LETTER "p"

pet pug

LETTER "p"

pat pet pig

LETTER "q"

quick quilt

LETTER "q"

quits quarry quest

LETTER "r"

raft rock

LETTER "r"

rat robs rings

LETTER "s"

sat sun

LETTER "s"

spill six sacks

LETTER "t"

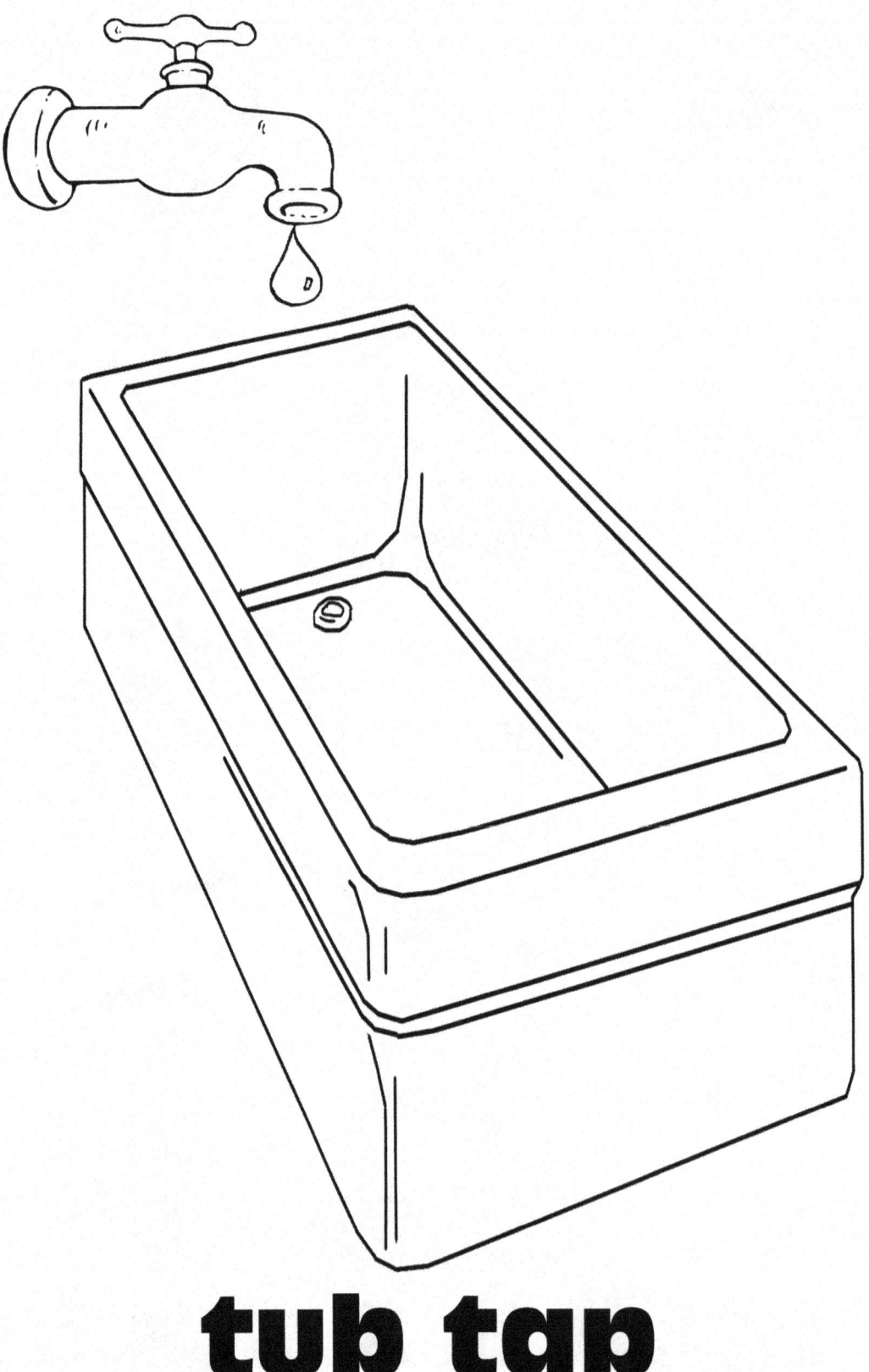

tub tap

LETTER "t"

ten tin tops

LETTER "u"

umbrella up

LETTER "u"

unbox ugly umbrellas

LETTER "v"

vet visit

LETTER "v"

velcro vest van

LETTER "w"

west wind

LETTER "w"

win wet wok

LETTER "x"

xmas unbox

LETTER "x"

xray ox ax

LETTER "y"

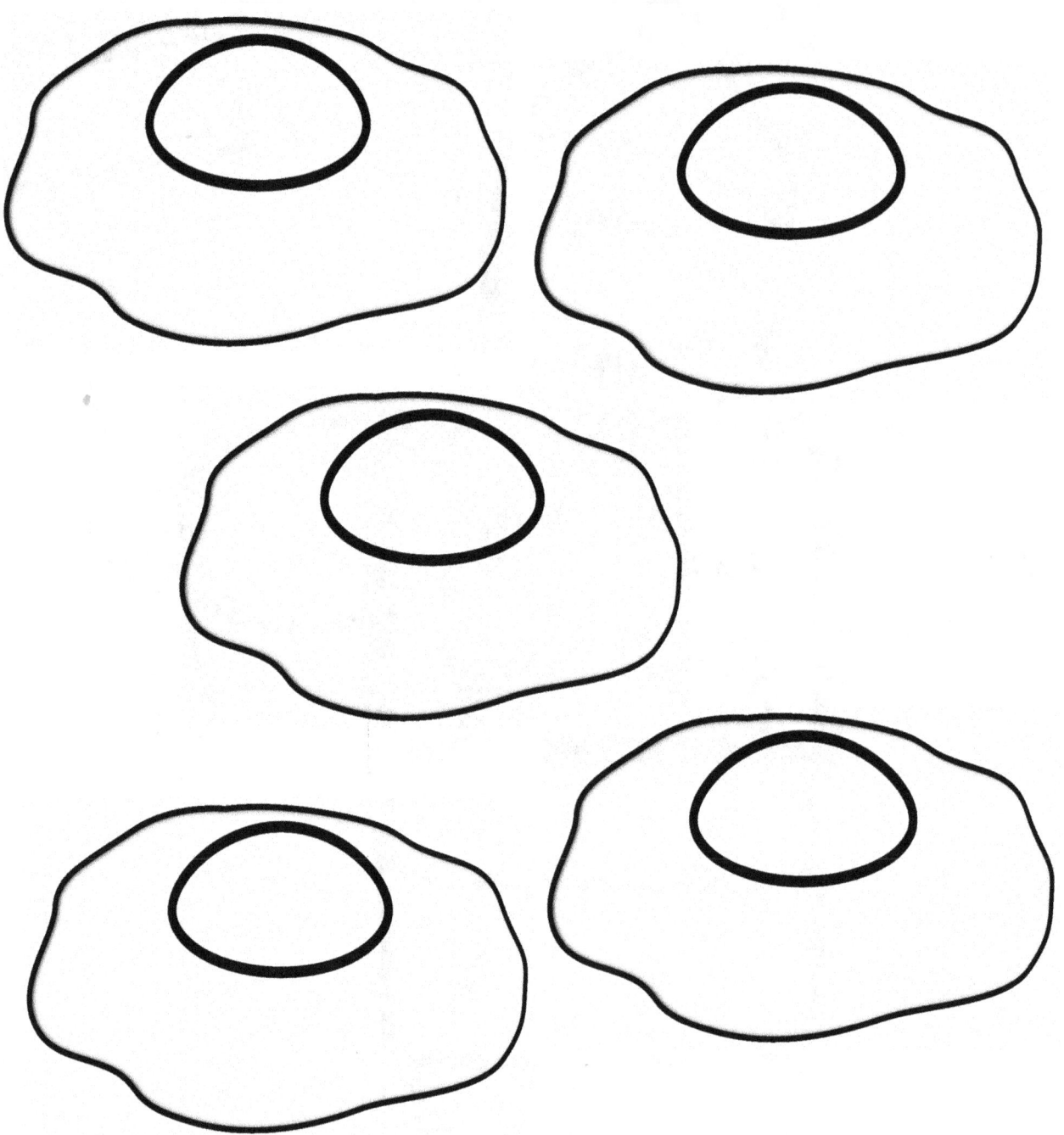

yellow yolks

LETTER "y"

yak yummy yams

LETTER "z"

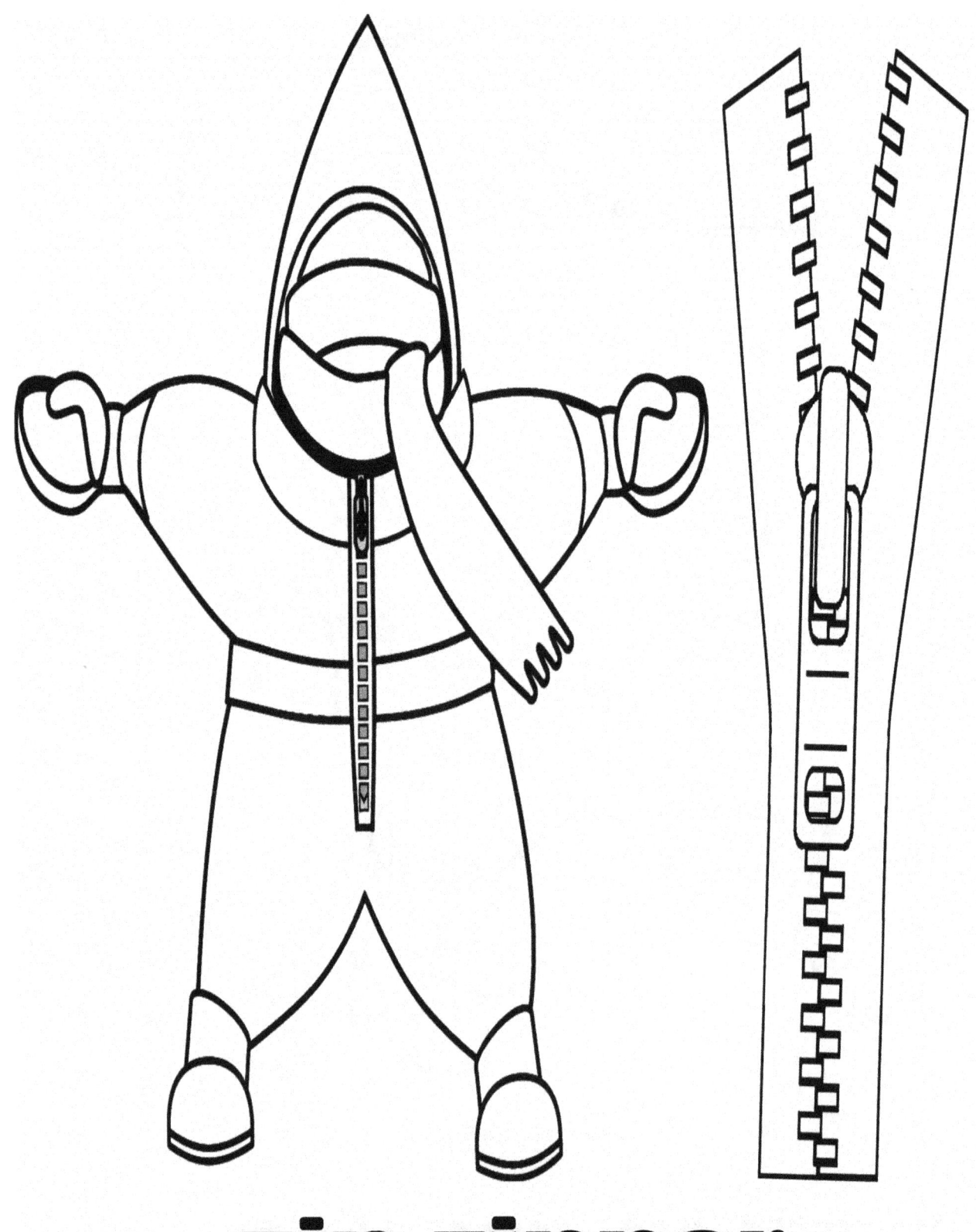

zip zipper

LETTER "z"

zebra zoo zest

LETTER SOUNDS – SIGHT WORDS "a"

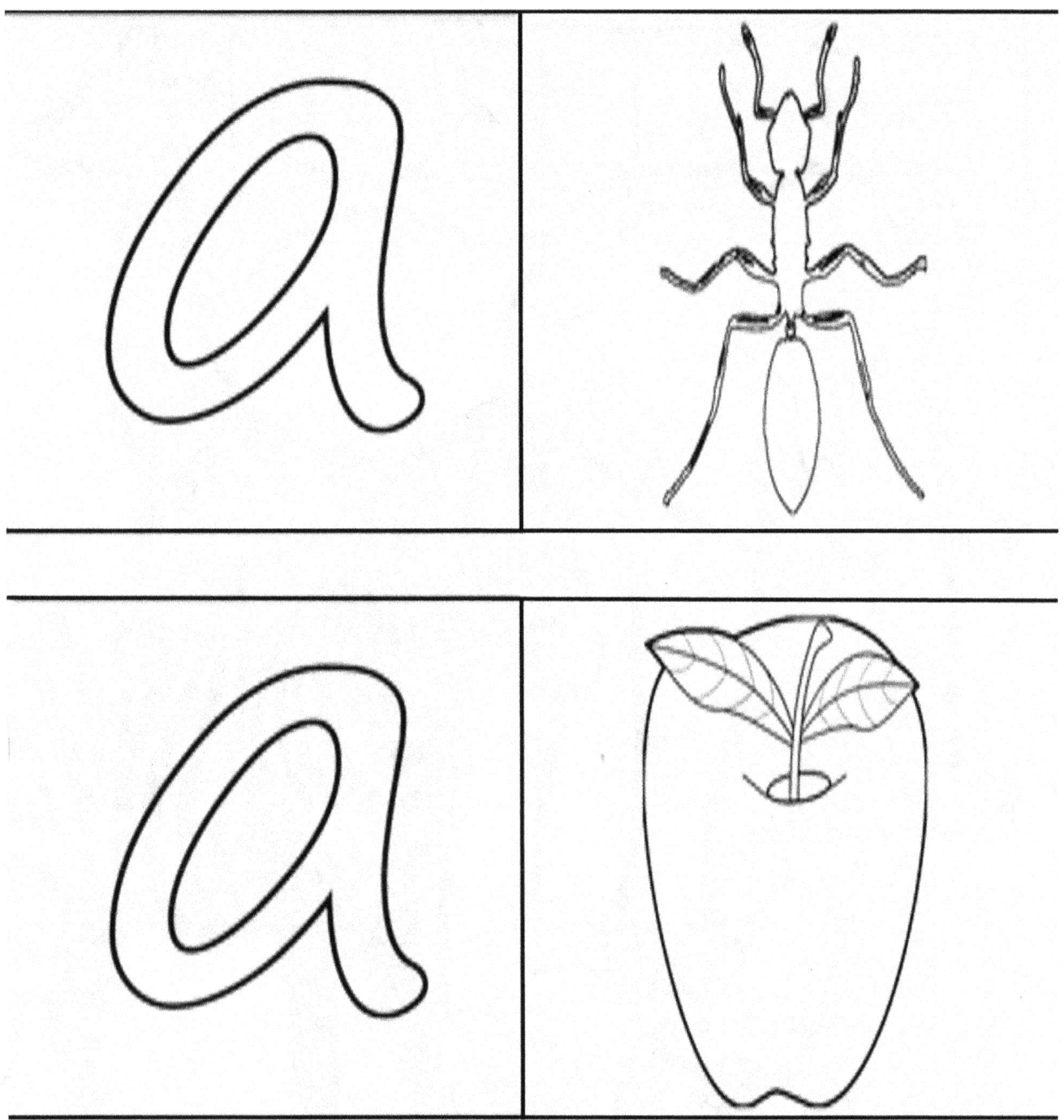

"a" as in "ant" or "apple".

SIGHT WORDS:

Pre-Primer: a, and, away.

Primer: all, am, are, at, ate.

LETTER SOUNDS – SIGHT WORDS "b"

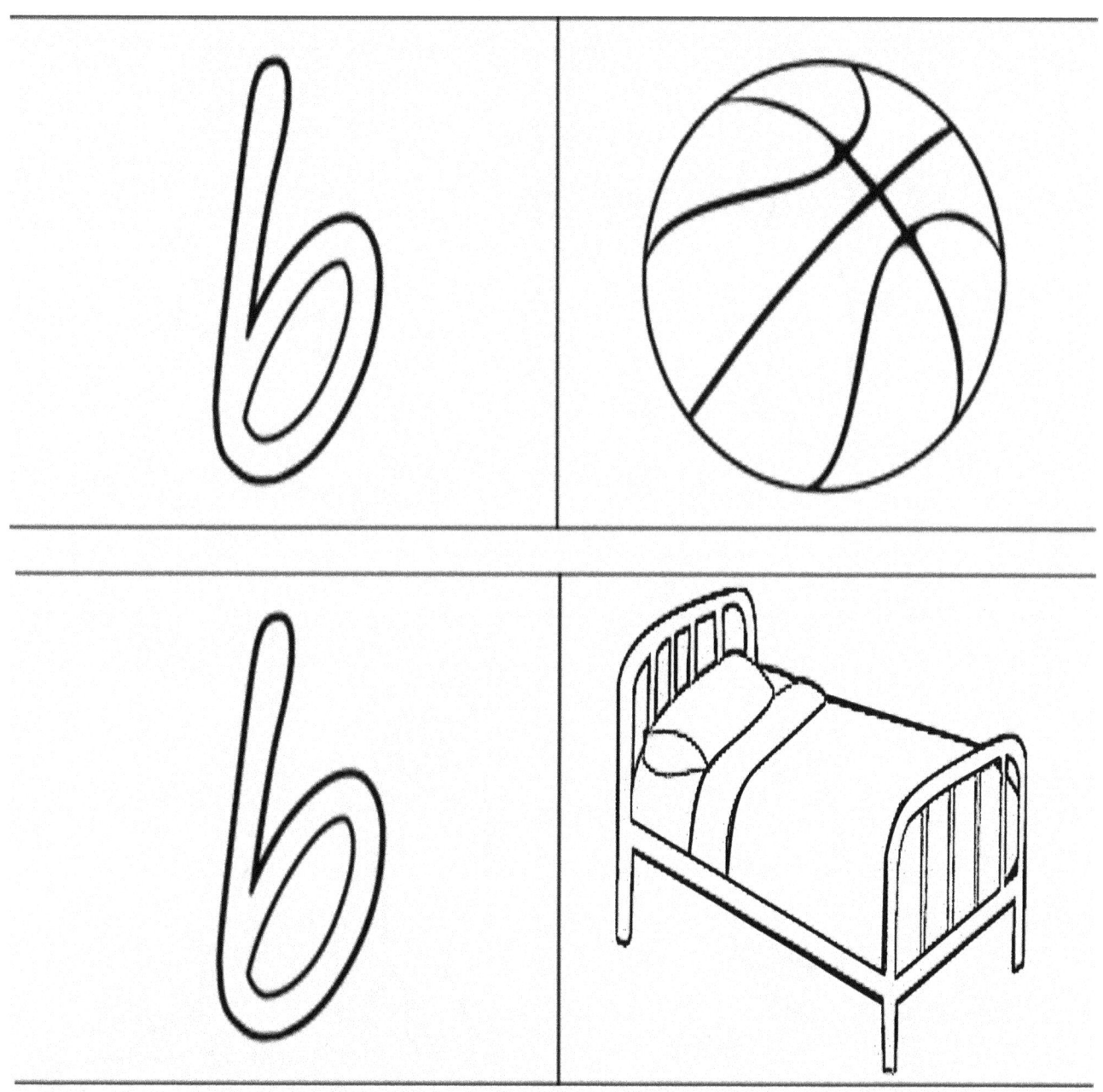

"b" as in "ball" and "bed"

SIGHT WORDS:

Pre-Primer: big, blue.

Primer: be, black, brown, but.

LETTER SOUNDS – SIGHT WORDS "c"

"c" as in "can" and "cat"

SIGHT WORDS:

Pre-Primer: can, come.

Primer: came.

LETTER SOUNDS – SIGHT WORDS "d"

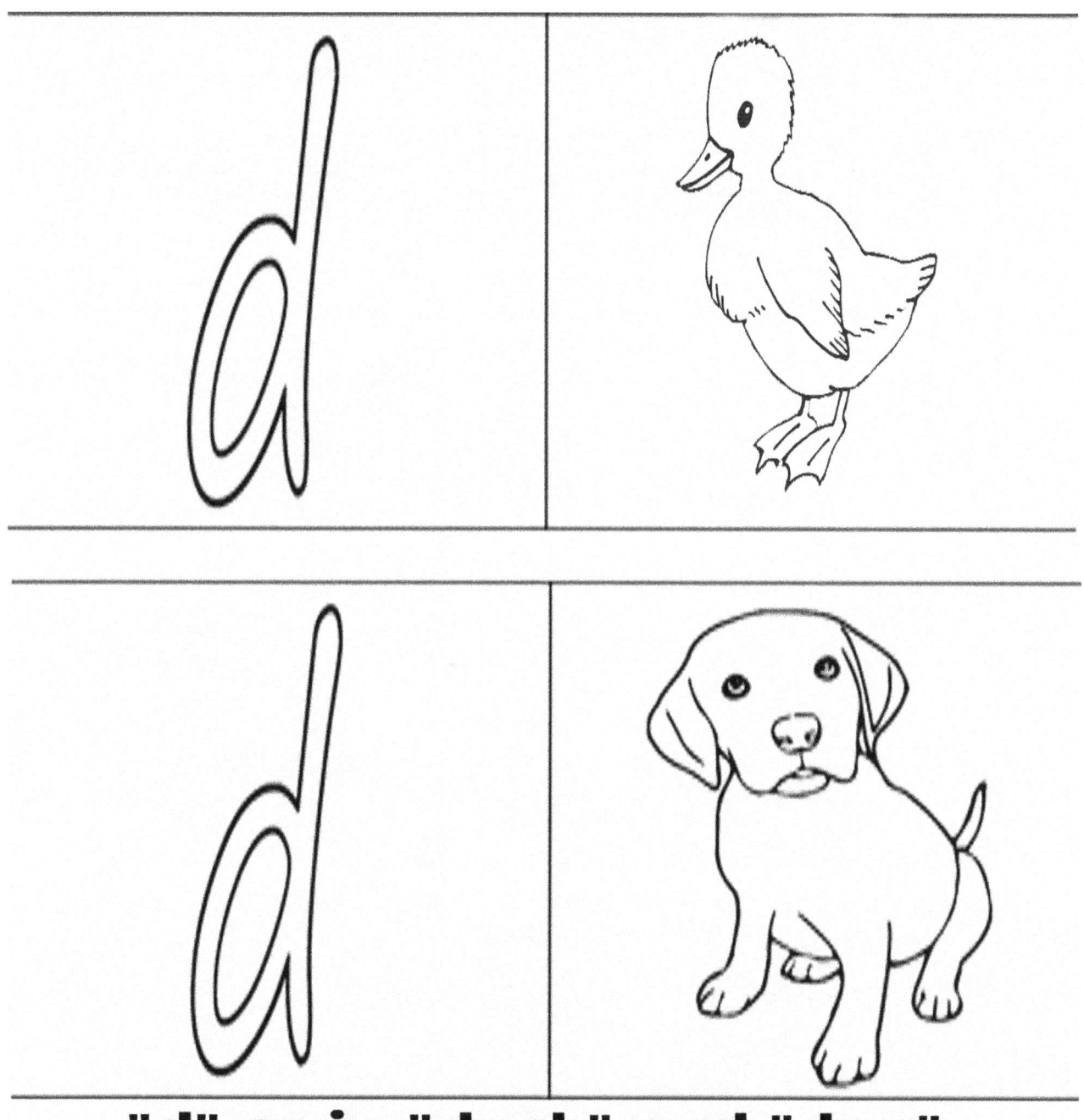

"d" as in "duck" and "dog"

SIGHT WORDS:

Pre-Primer: down.

Primer: did, do.

LETTER SOUNDS – SIGHT WORDS "e"

"e" as in "egg" and "engine"

SIGHT WORDS:

Pre-Primer:

Primer: eat.

LETTER SOUNDS – SIGHT WORDS "f"

"f" as in "fork" and "fridge"
SIGHT WORDS:

Pre-Primer: find, for, funny.

Primer: four.

LETTER SOUNDS – SIGHT WORDS "g"

"g" as in "glue" and "guitar"

SIGHT WORDS:

Pre-Primer: go.

Primer: get, good.

LETTER SOUNDS – SIGHT WORDS "h"

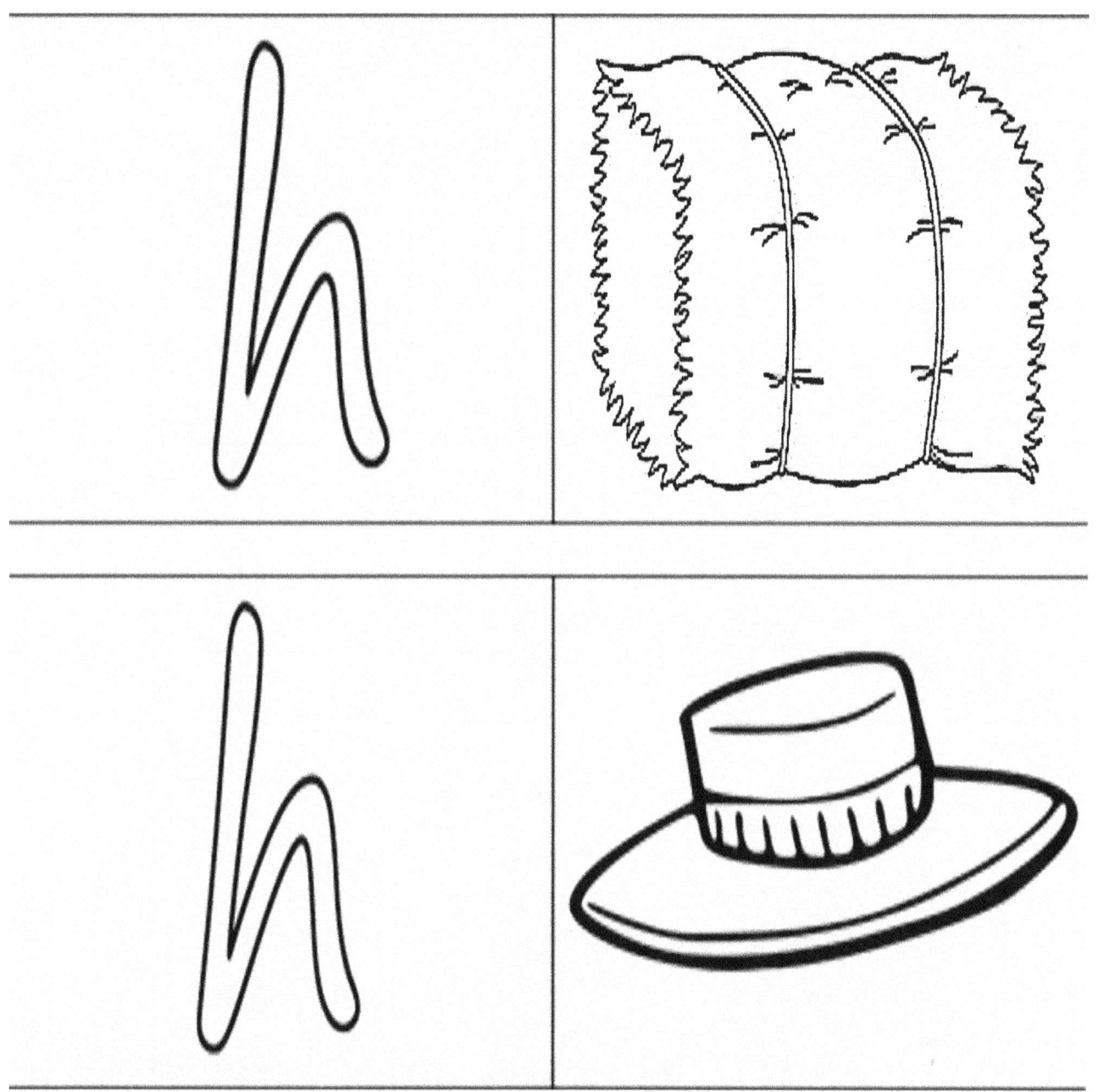

"h" as in "hay" and "hat"

SIGHT WORDS:

Pre-Primer: help, here.

Primer: have, he.

LETTER SOUNDS – SIGHT WORDS "i"

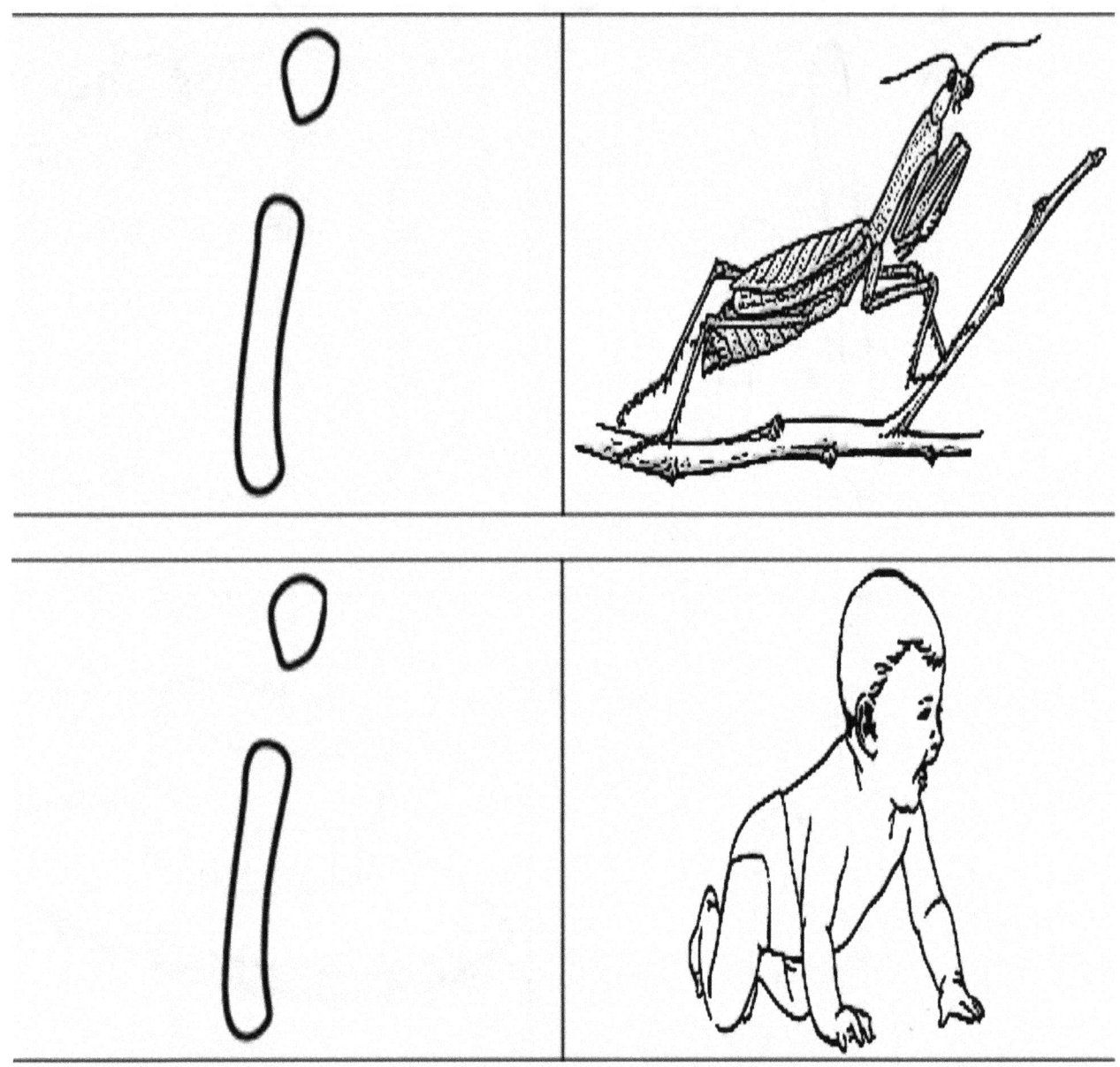

"i" as in "insect" and "infant"

SIGHT WORDS:

Pre-Primer: I, in, is, it.

Primer: into.

LETTER SOUNDS – SIGHT WORDS "j"

"j" as in "jar" and "juice"

SIGHT WORDS:

Pre-Primer: jump.

Primer:

LETTER SOUNDS – SIGHT WORDS "k"

"k" as in "key" and "kite"

SIGHT WORDS:

Pre-Primer:

Primer:

LETTER SOUNDS – SIGHT WORDS "l"

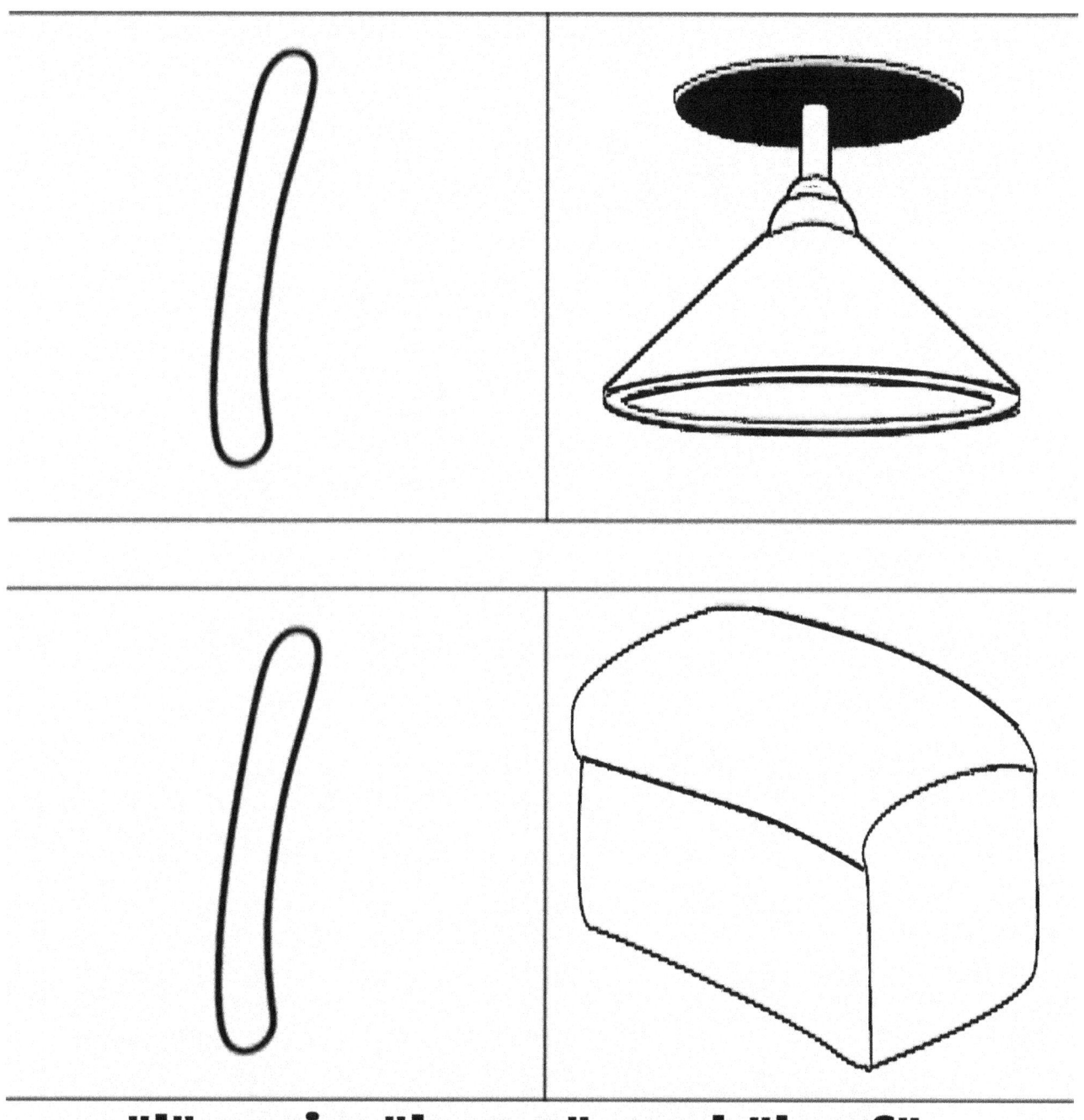

"l" as in "lamp" and "loaf"

SIGHT WORDS:

Pre-Primer: little, look.

Primer: like.

LETTER SOUNDS – SIGHT WORDS "m"

"m" as in "milk" and "mouse"

SIGHT WORDS:

Pre-Primer: make, me, my.

Primer: must.

LETTER SOUNDS – SIGHT WORDS "n"

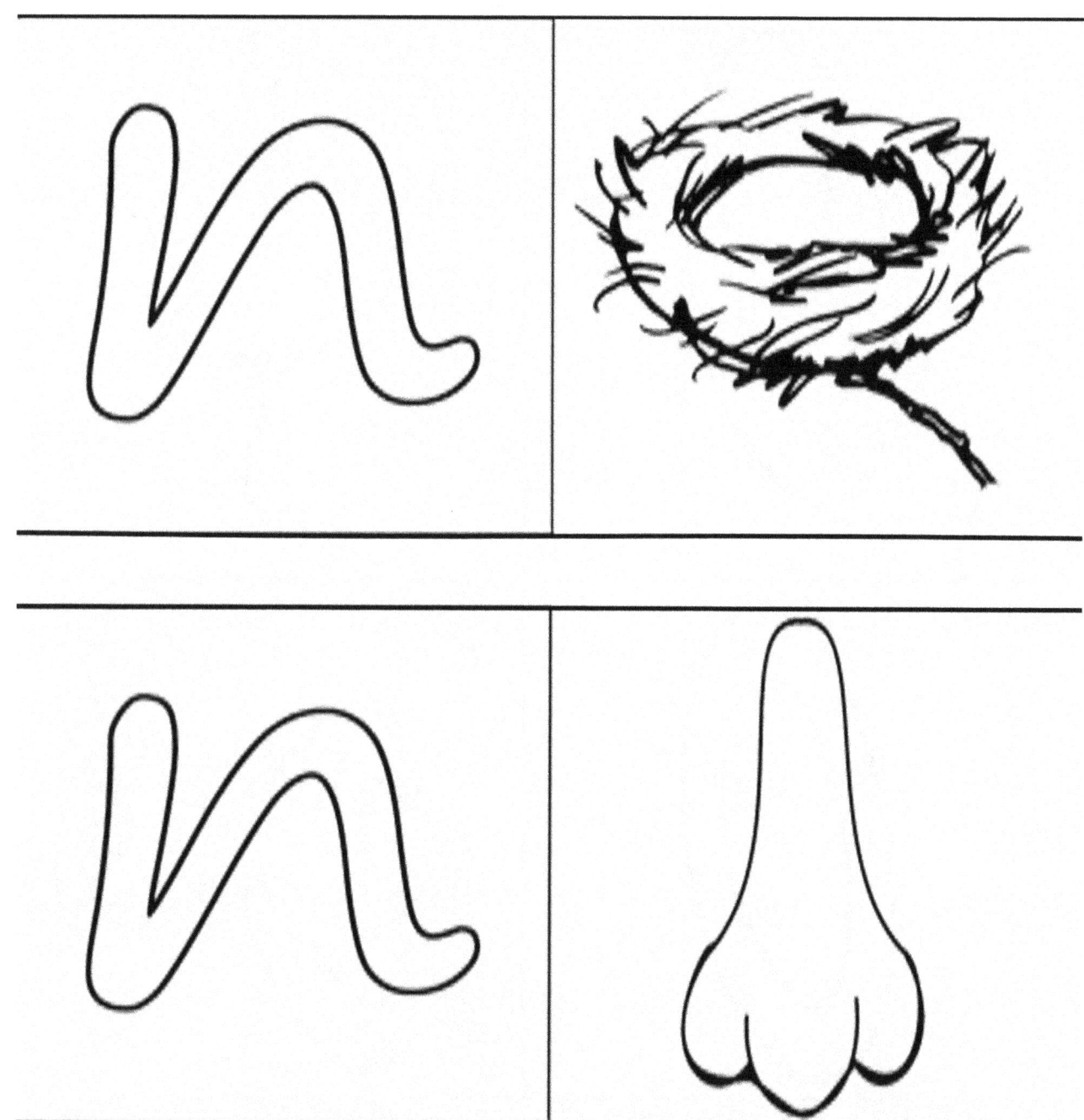

"n" as in "nest" and "nose"

SIGHT WORDS:
Pre-Primer: not.

Primer: new, no, now.

LETTER SOUNDS – SIGHT WORDS "o"

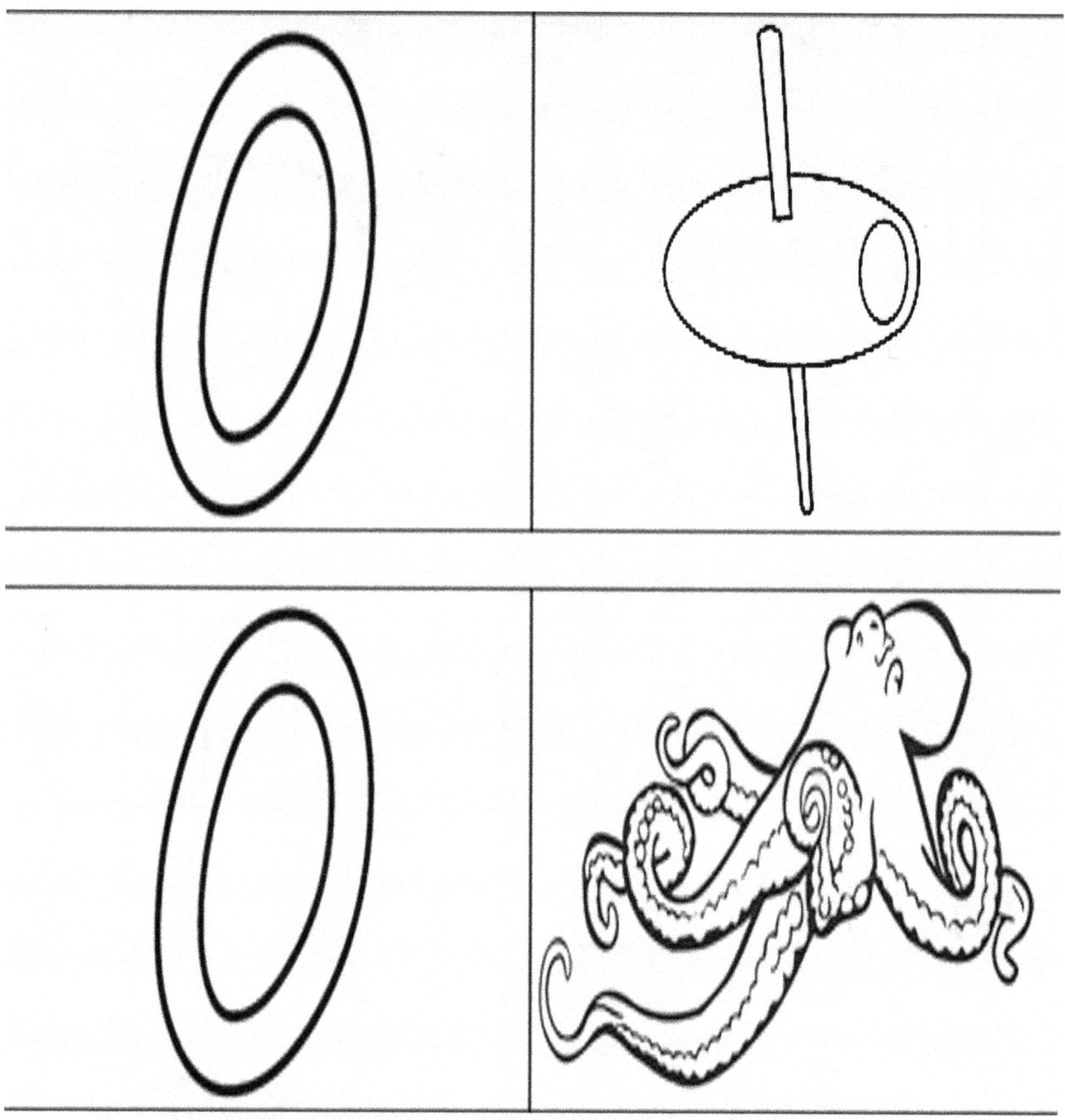

"o" as in "olive" and "octopus"

SIGHT WORDS:

Pre-Primer: one.

Primer: on, our, out.

LETTER SOUNDS – SIGHT WORDS "p"

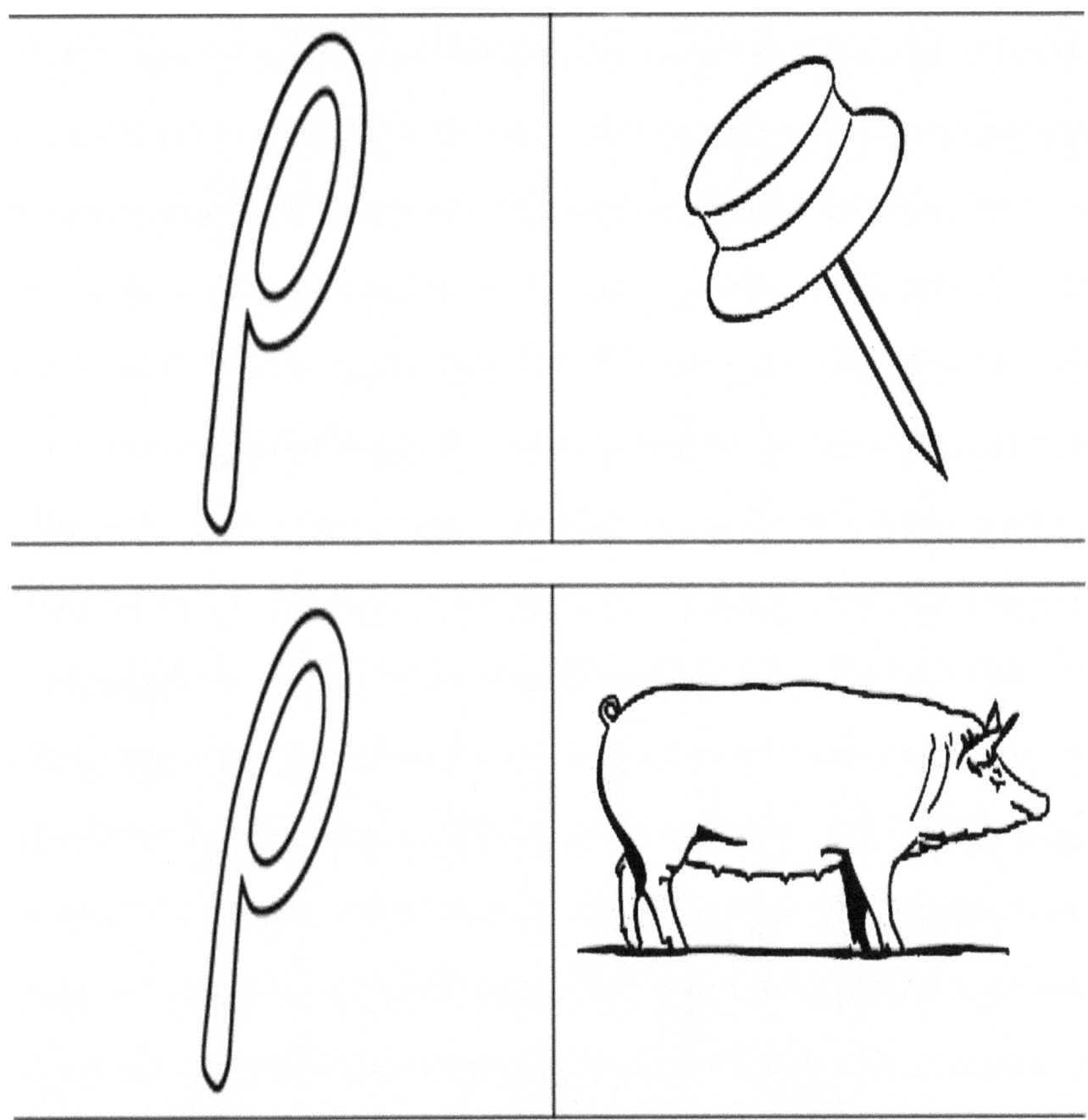

"p" as in "pin" and "pig"

SIGHT WORDS:

Pre-Primer: play.

Primer: please, pretty.

LETTER SOUNDS – SIGHT WORDS "q"

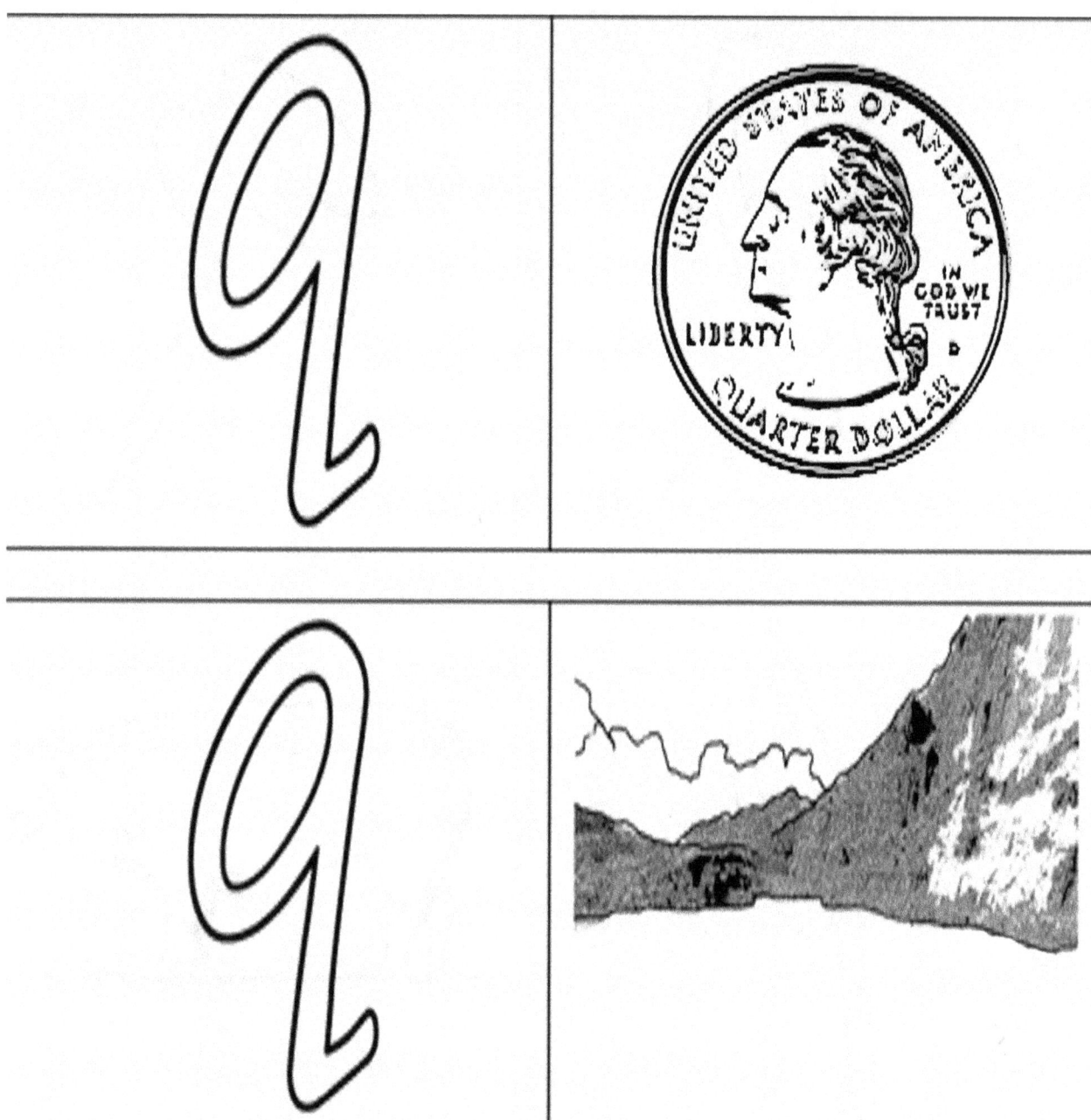

"q" as in "quarter" and "quarry"

SIGHT WORDS:

Pre-Primer:

Primer:

LETTER SOUNDS – SIGHT WORDS "r"

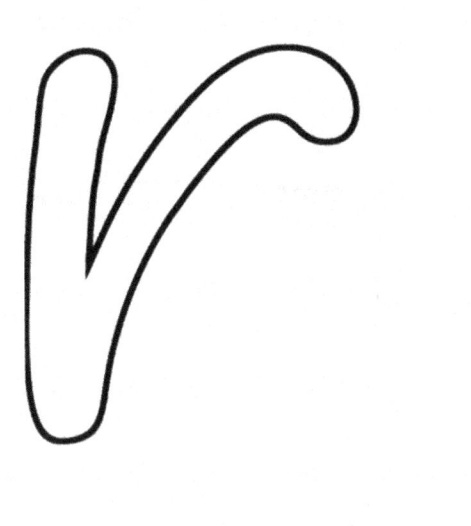 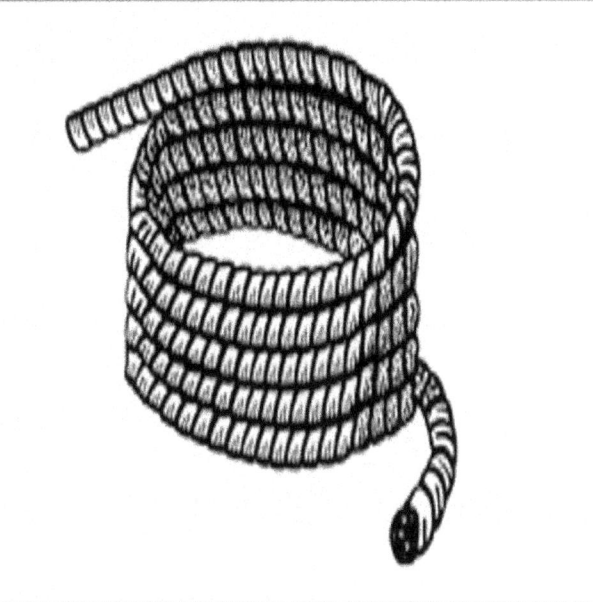

"r" as in "rope" and "rose"

SIGHT WORDS:

Pre-Primer: red, run.

Primer: ran, ride.

LETTER SOUNDS – SIGHT WORDS "s"

"s" as in "saw" and "sun"

SIGHT WORDS:

Pre-Primer: said, see.

Primer: saw, say, she, so, soon.

LETTER SOUNDS – SIGHT WORDS "t"

"t" as in "toilet" and "table"

SIGHT WORDS:

Pre-Primer: the, three, to, two.

Primer: that, there, they, this, too.

LETTER SOUNDS – SIGHT WORDS "u"

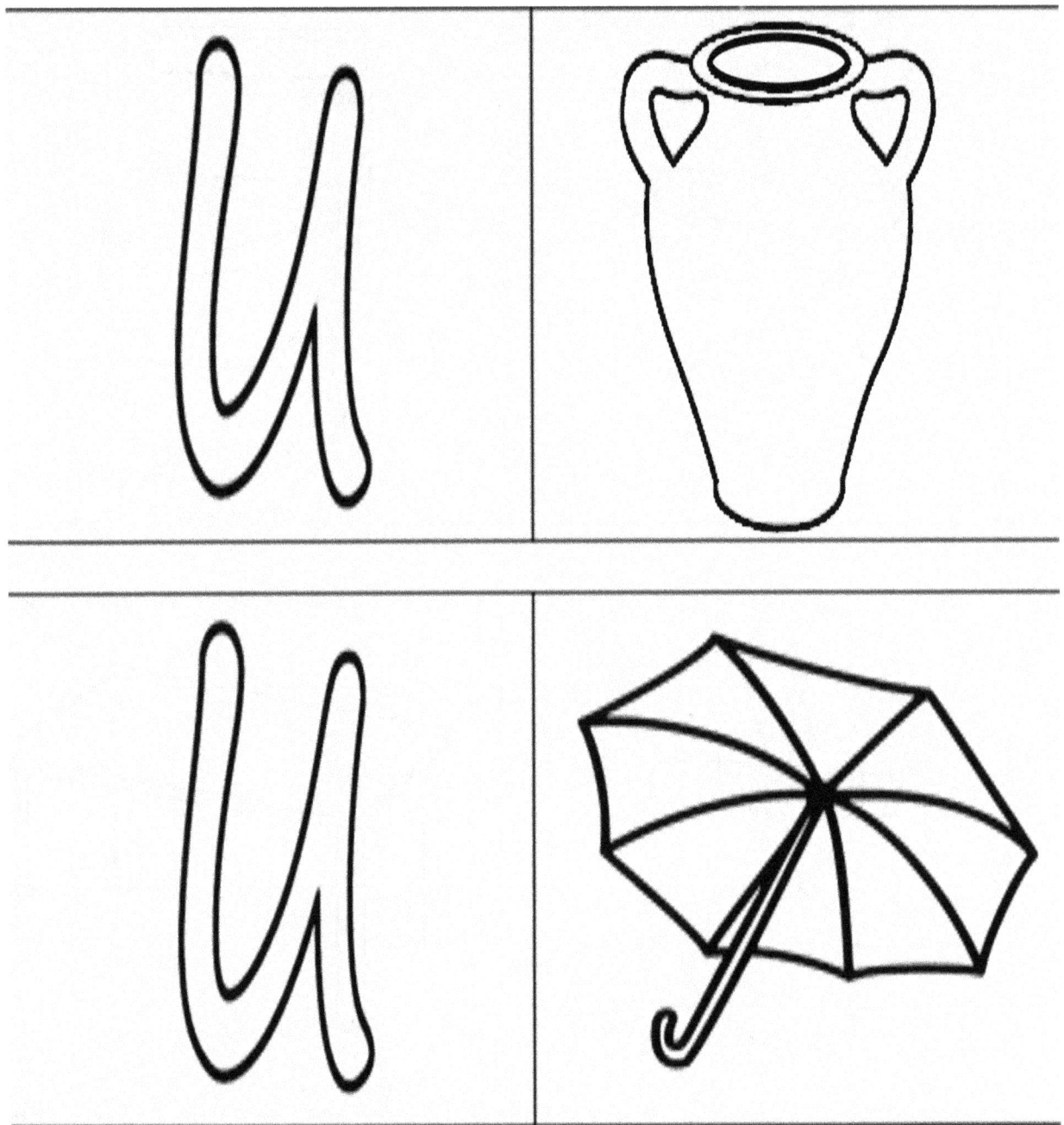

"u" as in "urn" and "umbrella"

SIGHT WORDS:

Pre-Primer: up.

Primer: under.

LETTER SOUNDS – SIGHT WORDS "v"

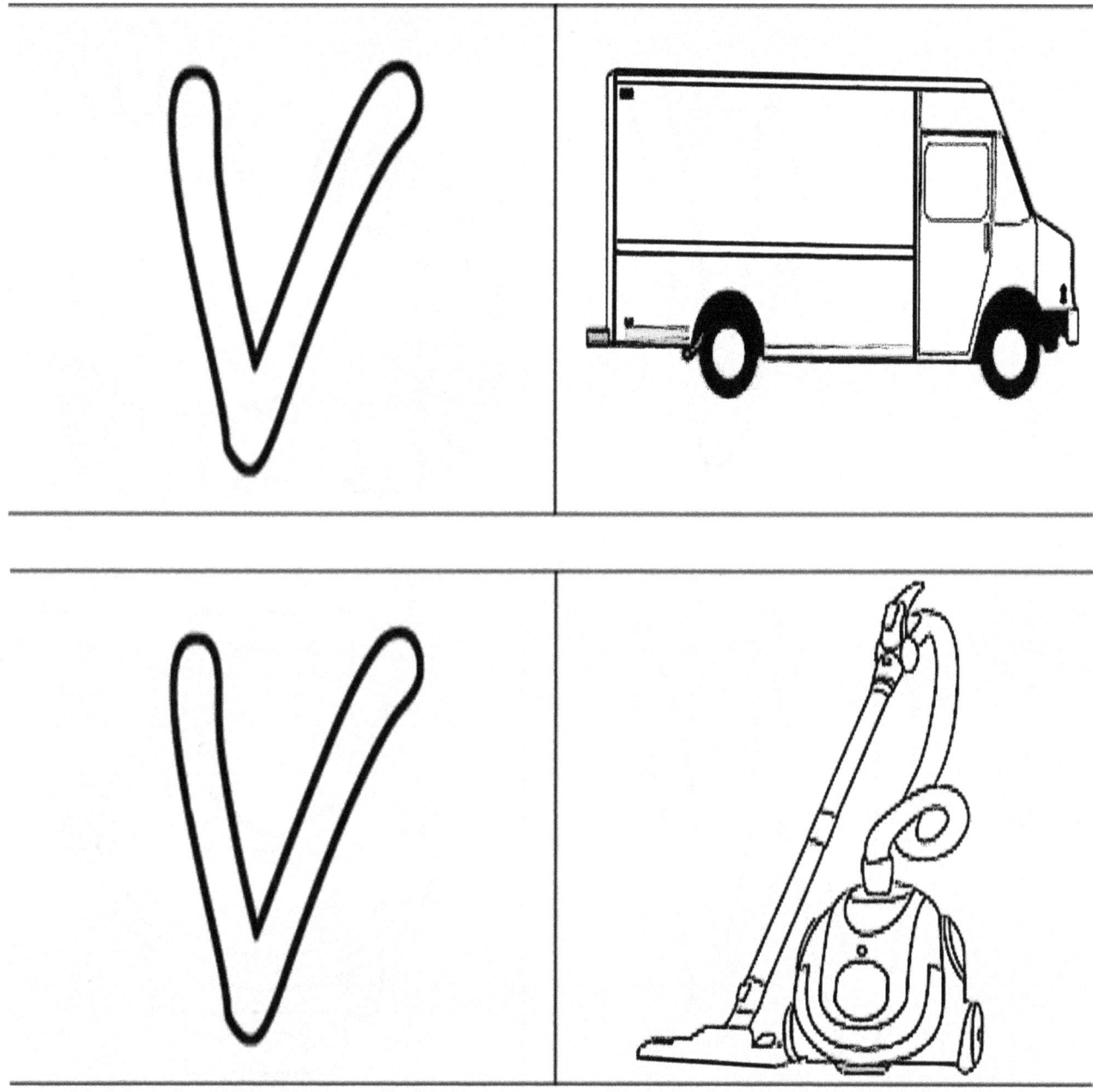

"v" as in "van" and "vacuum"
SIGHT WORDS:
Pre-Primer:

Primer:

LETTER SOUNDS – SIGHT WORDS "w"

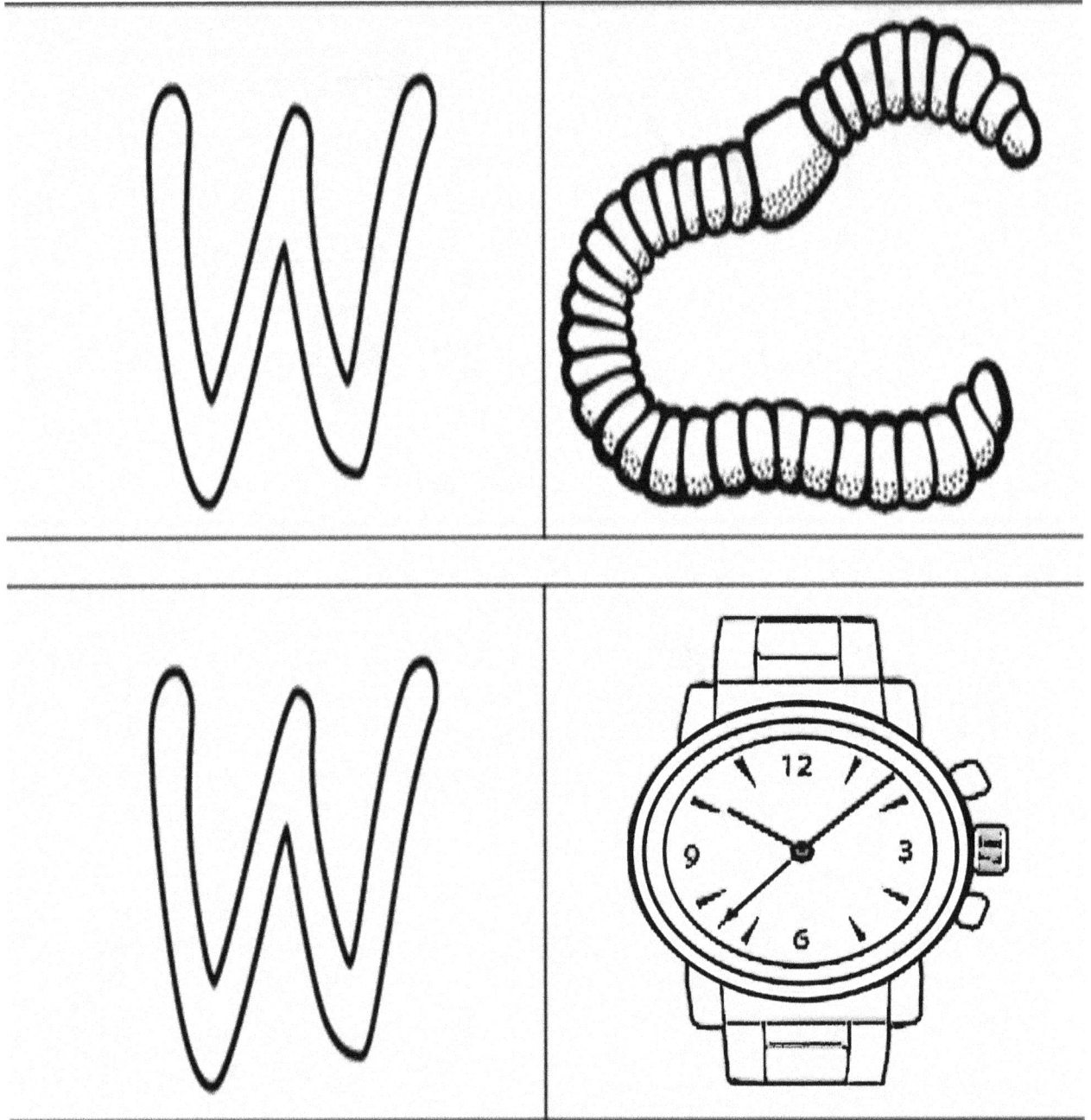

"w" as in "worm" and "watch"

SIGHT WORDS:

Pre-Primer: we, where, want, was, well.

Primer: went, what, white, who, will, with.

LETTER SOUNDS – SIGHT WORDS "x"

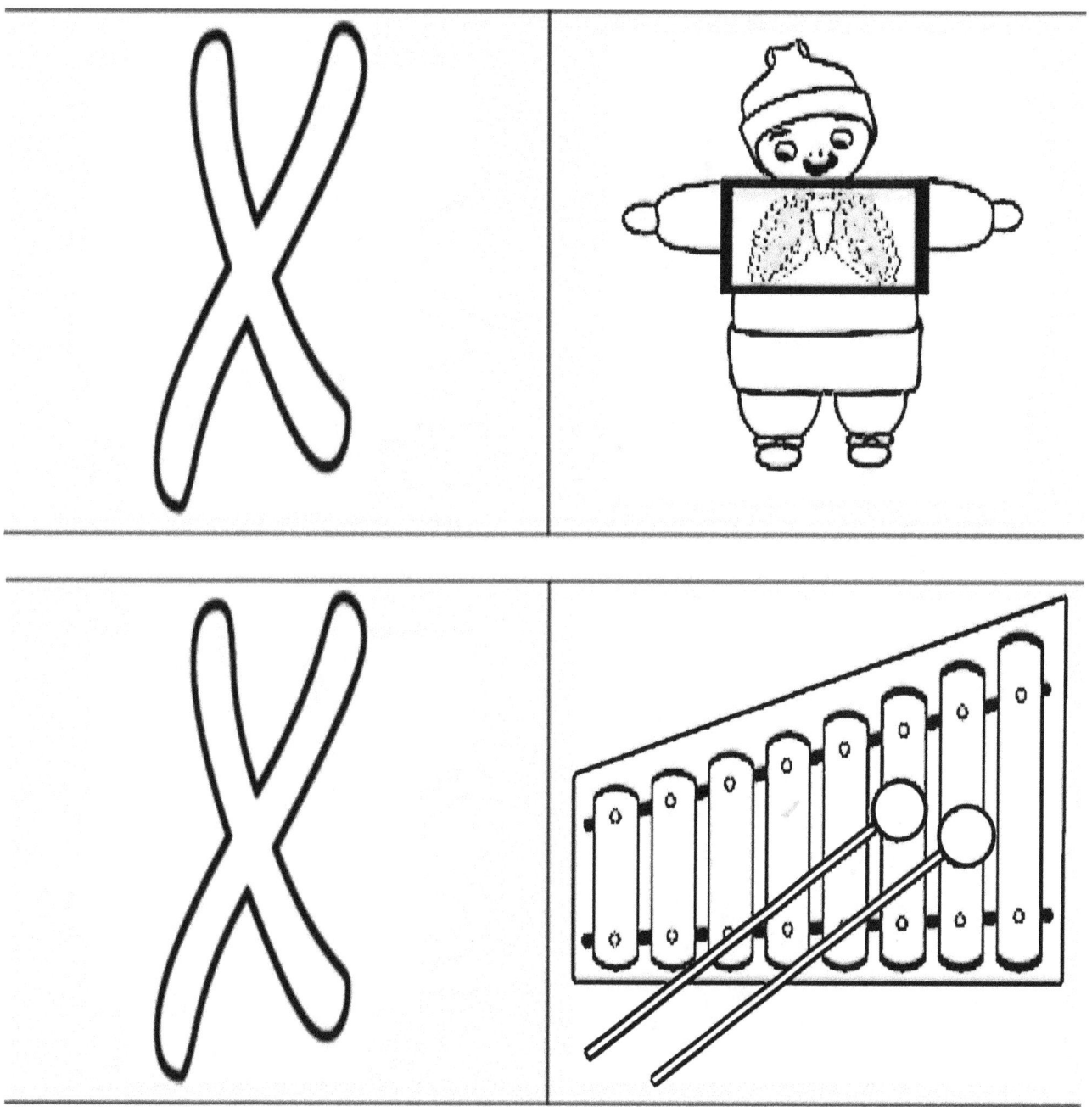

"x" as in "x-ray" and "xylophone"

SIGHT WORDS:

Pre-Primer:

Primer:

LETTER SOUNDS – SIGHT WORDS "y"

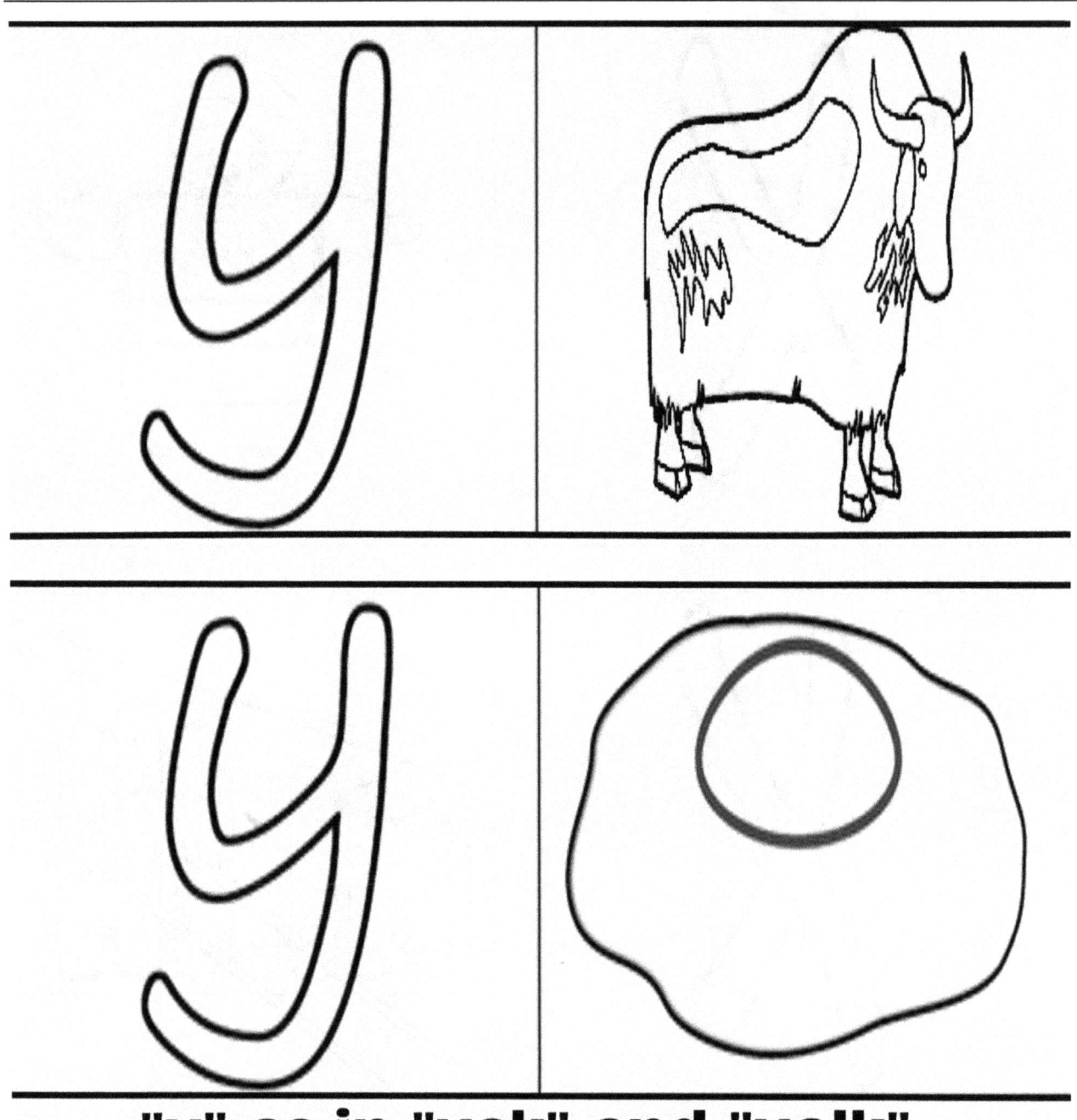

"y" as in "yak" and "yolk"

SIGHT WORDS:

Pre-Primer: yellow, you.

Primer: yes.

LETTER SOUNDS – SIGHT WORDS "z"

"z" as in "zebra" and "zoo"

SIGHT WORDS:

Pre-Primer:

Primer:

OTHER BOOKS BY THE AUTHOR

Buy these books at: http://howtoteachchildrentoread.ca

	**HOW TO TEACH CHILDREN TO READ** This book introduces children to 86 phonetic sounds of the English language in a step by step plan to teach a child of any age to read. How To Teach Children To Read also introduces the 220 Dolch word list (sight words) so that a child will be able to read, write and spell most written words.
	**TEACH YOUR CHILD TO READ – ALPHABET AND THREE LETTER WORDS** This book introduces 26 alphabet letter sounds and shows children how to read and write three letter words. A preschool child learns the 26 basic phonetic sounds of the English alphabet; how to read and write most three letter words; and that alphabet letter sounds form words written in books.
	**TEACH YOUR CHILD TO READ – VOWELS-PHONICS and SIGHT WORDS** This book is the second step in a preschool child learning to read. Children will learn 60 blended phonetic sounds; 220 Dolch Sight Words; how to read and write three, four or more letter words using a play-based method to teach a preschool child how to read.
	**TEACH YOUR CHILD TO READ – ALPHABET PHONICS SHORT SENTENCES** Third Book in the "Teach Your Child To Read" series. Children learn how alphabet sounds form words; how to read three - and four-letter words; how to read short sentences; the most common Sight Words; blended consonant sounds and that reading can be fun.

OTHER BOOKS BY THE AUTHOR
Buy these books at: http://howtoteachchildrentoread.ca

	**PLAY-BASED WAYS TO TEACH YOUR CHILD TO READ** This book shows you what play based toys and learning to read materials to use; a step by step plan to teach your child to read and write; how to present learning to read materials to your child; how to set up the in home reading and writing environment; that preschool children can learn to read and write.
	**LEO LEARNS TO READ** A "Teach Your Child To Read Story." Join Leo the lion on a journey to the library with his jungle friends; on the way to the library, Leo hides a secret he does not want his friends to know. Children learn the fundamentals keys of reading, and that learning to read helps us read to learn. An ideal picture story to read to your children to help them learn about reading.
	**ALPHABET PARK – A STORY TEACHING CHILDREN HOW TO READ** This story book teaches children the alphabet; what alphabet letters sound like; that letter sounds form words and words describe things; that nouns are the names of things; how to use imagination; communication skills; about feelings and values; developmental movement activities; starting to write the letter sounds; starting to write pre-primer Sight Words.
	**A WALK IN THE JUNGLE** Prepare preschool children emotionally, intellectually and physically, before they go to grade school. Give your child an unprecedented, LIFELONG advantage, simply by reading them a storybook; a storybook UNLIKE ANY OTHER you've seen before. It feels so good to see your child achieve milestones, absorb knowledge like a sponge and develop a true love of learning.

OTHER BOOKS BY THE AUTHOR
Buy these books at: http://howtoteachchildrentoread.ca

	**GORDY VISITS THE MOUTAINS** Gordy Visits The Mountains: helps children develop physical coordination, improves self-direction, enhances decision making, promotes problem solving. A fun play-based child development storybook activity gets your child ready to learn.
	**ALPHABETIC PHONICS - FAST START FOR EARLY READERS LEVEL 1** Once a pre-school child has learned the 26-alphabet letter sounds, 60 phonogram blended consonant sounds and the Pre-primer Sight Words, it is time to introduce short sentence readers of two, three, four or more words. In Alphabetic Phonics - Fast Start For Early Readers Level 1 children sound out the alphabet letter sounds to form two and three letter words. This book also contains the 26 phonic alphabet letter sounds, as well as the pre and primer Sight Words for each letter of the alphabet.
	**ALPHABETIC PHONICS - FAST START FOR EARLY READERS LEVEL 2** Children have learned to sound out and read two and three letter words in level 1, in level 2 they are introduced to four or more words; capitals; punctation of a sentence; and pre and primer Sight Words to create sentences.
	**EDUCATIONAL CHILD'S PLAY** Play-based Child Development Activities. Prepare pre-school children emotionally, intellectually and physically, before they start school. A book jammed packed with play-based child development activities.

OTHER BOOKS BY THE AUTHOR
Buy these books at: http://howtoteachchildrentoread.ca

	**PRE SCHOOL COLORING AND PUZZLE BOOK** This coloring book is designed to help pre-school children with the following possible benefits: increase creativity; a free time activity; a transitional activity; a soothing distraction; improve fine motor skills; calm and center the mind; stimulate the brain and the senses; help focus the mind in the moment; take the mind off distracting thoughts.
	**ADULT AND CHILDREN COLORING BOOK** A 128 page adult and children coloring and puzzle book. The pictures and puzzles are printable for any age group, from adult coloring to children. This book was designed for my 42 year old daughter who had a stroke, and has limited movement and communication due to her stroke. This book is helping her use both hands, better her fine motor skills, and improve logical thinking skills.
	**MOTIVATIONAL COLORING PUZZLE BOOK** This book has inspirational pictures, comic art, and puzzles for children, adults and seniors. It is the Author's hope readers may experience some of the following benefits: Give children a calming activity. Help children learn to read and write. Increase your creativity. Challenge your thinking skills. Reduce stress. Improve your state of wellness. Improve fine motor skills. Calm and center the mind in the moment.
	**WORKPLACE STRESS MANAGEMENT** Do you feel stressed and anxious at work? You're about to discover easy to do workplace stress management activities to reduce stress, anxiety, and the possibility of a nervous breakdown in the workplace. You will Learn: a 5-minute exercise to start and finish your day; practical, easy to learn movements to help reduce workplace stress and anxiety.

OTHER BOOKS BY THE AUTHOR
Buy these books at: http://howtoteachchildrentoread.ca

	**GETTING THROUGH YOUR DAY** Getting Through Your Day Motivational Activities to help you reduce stress, be alert, in the moment, energized, and living a full life. This book introduces you to a 5-minute movement-based exercise to start your day. You will learn to focus the mind, energize the body, and be ready for a meaningful day.
	**FUN DAY FOR SENIORS** Thousands of activities to help seniors be alert, in the moment, energized and living a full life.

ABOUT THE AUTHOR

The author (Paul Mackie) has over twenty years of experience working with children and adults as an educator, and personal care worker.

Paul is a certified Early Childhood Educator in British Columbia, and a level two Early Childhood Educator in Alberta Canada.

Paul has worked as a Community Care worker with special needs children, adults and seniors; and has worked with children in daycares, day programs, and the school system.

The author has had several careers, with certification as a Marine Engineer; Industrial Millwright, Welder; Early Childhood Educator; with experience as a Teacher's Assistant; special needs childcare worker; Brain Gym Instructor; Senior Building Manager; with courses of study such as "The Writing Road to Reading", "Accelerated Learning" and other brain development courses.

The author is now retired from his last position as Senior Building Manager for a non-profit housing society.

http://howtoteachchildrentoread.ca